FLIGHT

HOW IT WORKS

FLIGHT

BILL GUNSTON

Cavendish Square

Published in 2025 by Cavendish Square Publishing, LLC
2544 Clinton Street, Buffalo, NY 14224

Website: cavendishsq.com

Series editor: Elizabeth Miles
Cover design: Duck Egg Blue
Illustrations: Ian Howatson and Sebastian Quigley
Photographs: Arpingstone, Shutterstock.com (Mikado767, KITTIPHONG PHONGAEN, Skycolors, 1989studio, Mikhail Starodubov, desertfox99, Peter Baxter, topseller, Iakov Filimonov, Gary L. Brewer, Everett Collection, christopher babcock, Kletr, Skycolors, ra.photo, Fasttailwind, Newcastle, Soonthorn Wongsaita, Ewa Studio, Sufi, Martijn Smeets, Olga Gabay, Steve Mann, arogant)

Cataloging-in-Publication Data

Names: Gunston, Bill.
Title: Flight / Bill Gunston.
Description: Buffalo, NY : Cavendish Square Publishing, 2025. |
Series: How it works | Includes index.
Identifiers: ISBN 9781502671882 (pbk.) | ISBN 9781502671899 (library bound) |
ISBN 9781502671905 (ebook)
Subjects: LCSH: Flight--Juvenile literature. | Aeronautics--Juvenile literature. |
Aerodynamics--Juvenile literature.
Classification: LCC TL547.G84 2025 | DDC 629.13--dc23

CPSIA compliance information: Batch #CSCSQ25: For further information contact Cavendish Square Publishing LLC at 1-877-980-4450.

Printed in the United States of America

Contents

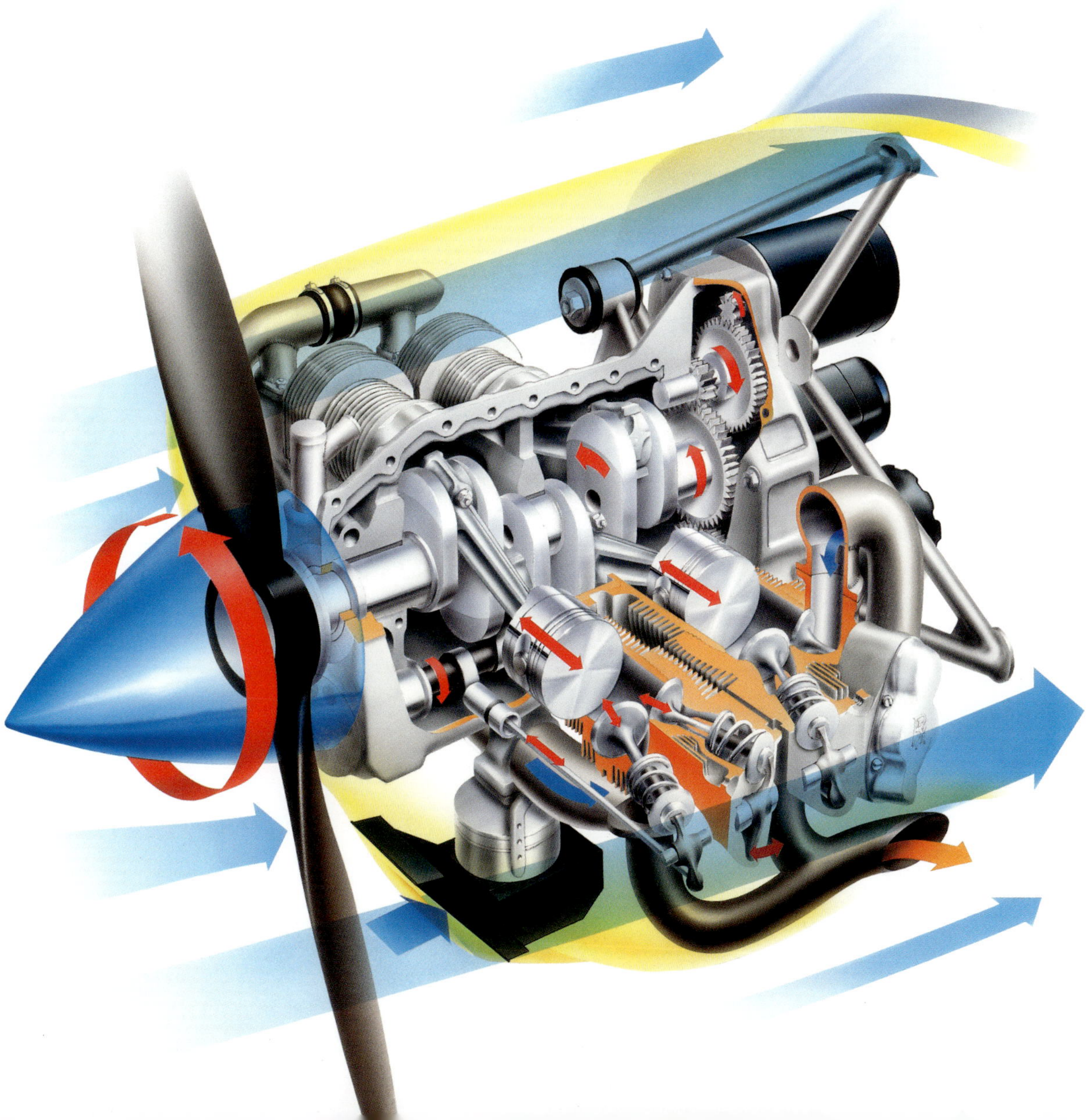

Balloons

Over 200 years ago, in 1783, two French men, Joseph and Etienne Montgolfier, invented the first hot-air balloon. Hot air rises because it has a lower density than cold air. The hot, lower-density air inside a hot-air balloon makes the balloon lighter than the cooler, higher-density air around it, which forces the balloon to rise.

Today, many people enjoy ballooning as a leisure activity. Balloonists are carried in a strong but light basket suspended beneath the balloon. The basket also holds tanks of liquid fuel, called propane, which feed a burner. The burner sends a long flame into the balloon to heat the air inside, gently lifting it to flying altitude. The balloon then floats along, carried by the wind. From time to time, the air inside has to be heated up again by switching on the burner. If the balloon's air is not reheated, the balloon will begin to descend.

Montgolfier

In 1783, the Montgolfier balloon (*above*) carried the first people on an air flight of any kind. Cords supported the wickerwork gallery at the bottom and chains held the brazier under the envelope. The Montgolfier brothers did not realize it was the hot air from the brazier that made it fly; they thought that the brazier produced a special gas that made the balloon rise.

Hydrogen balloon

Pictured left is one of the first balloons to be filled with a low-density gas, instead of hot air. Hydrogen is the lightest of all gases, so it gives the most powerful lift. Unlike a hot-air balloon, a hydrogen balloon does not need a burner. The first pioneering flights in hydrogen balloons were made over 200 years ago.

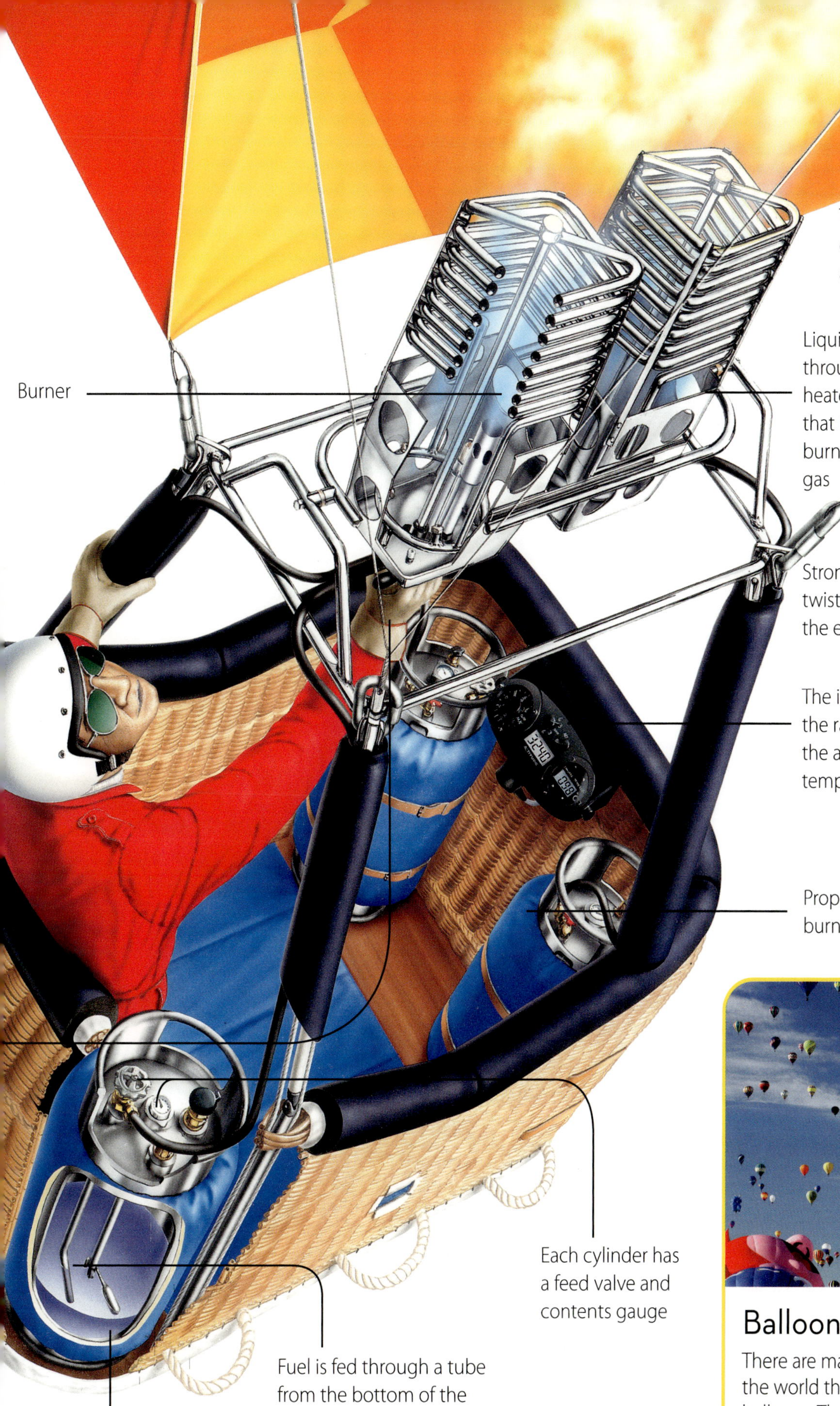

Balloon festivals

There are many festivals across the world that celebrate hot-air balloons. The largest is in New Mexico (*above*), where thousands of people visit to see hundreds of balloons of all shapes and sizes.

Airships

Hot-air balloons are blown wherever the wind takes them. Airships were invented so that the direction of travel could be controlled. Early airships consisted of an envelope with a rigid frame, which contained separate gas bags. Today, airships are nonrigids, or "blimps," which means they have an envelope made of flexible fabric, like a balloon. Helium gas fills most of the envelope. Helium is less dense, and therefore lighter, than air, so it lifts the airship. The gondola, or cabin, of this nonrigid airship (*right*) carries two piston engines, which drive propellers inside ducts. The ducts can be rotated to make the propellers push the airship forward, up, or down.

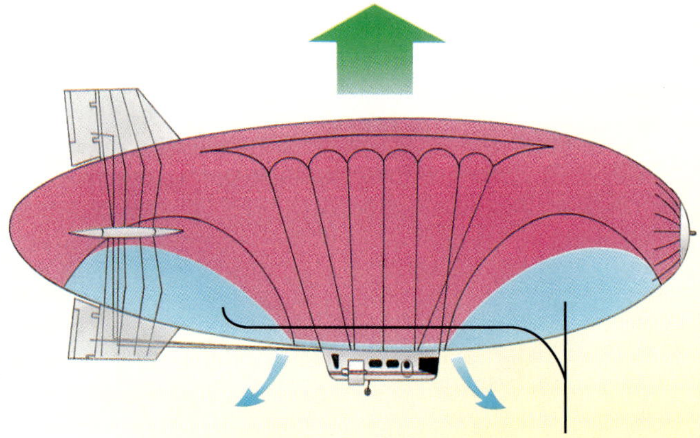

Modern airships

Most of the envelope contains helium, which lifts the weight of the airship. But two large bags, called ballonets, contain air. For the airship to rise or fall, air is pumped out of (*above*) or into (*above right*) the ballonets.

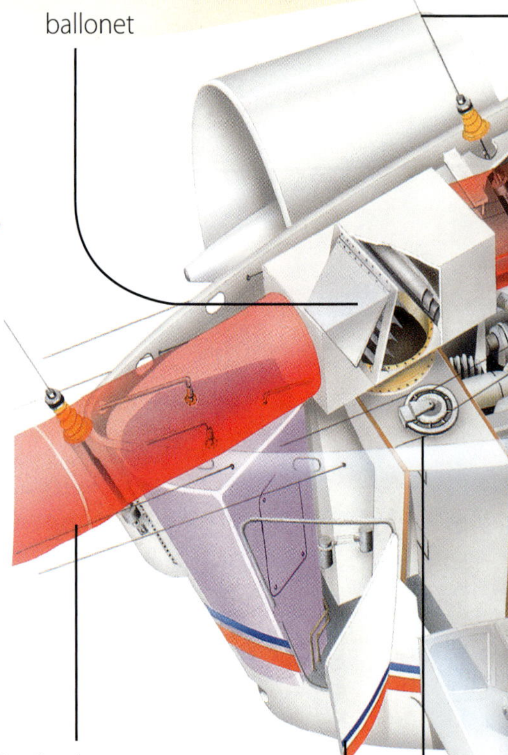

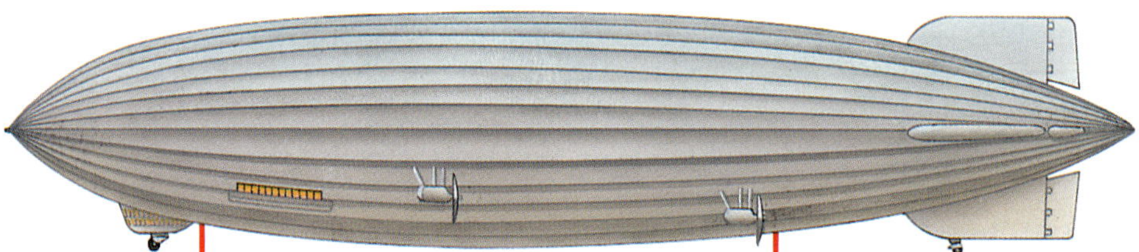

LZ 129 Hindenburg

The *Hindenburg* (*above*) was the largest flying machine ever built. First flown in 1936, it was a rigid airship and had 25 double bedrooms for passengers. This hydrogen-filled airship was destroyed by fire in 1937 (*below*).

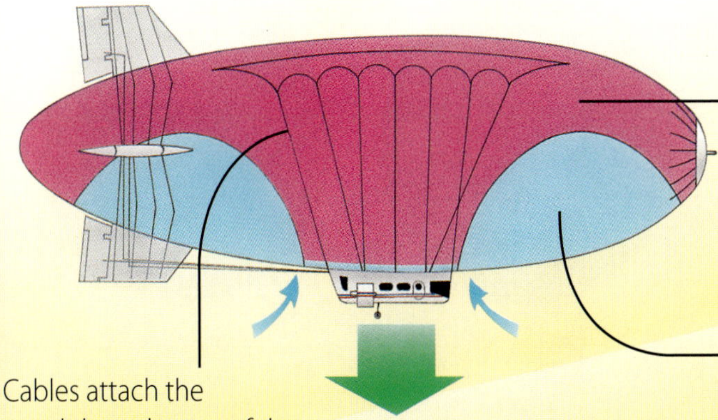

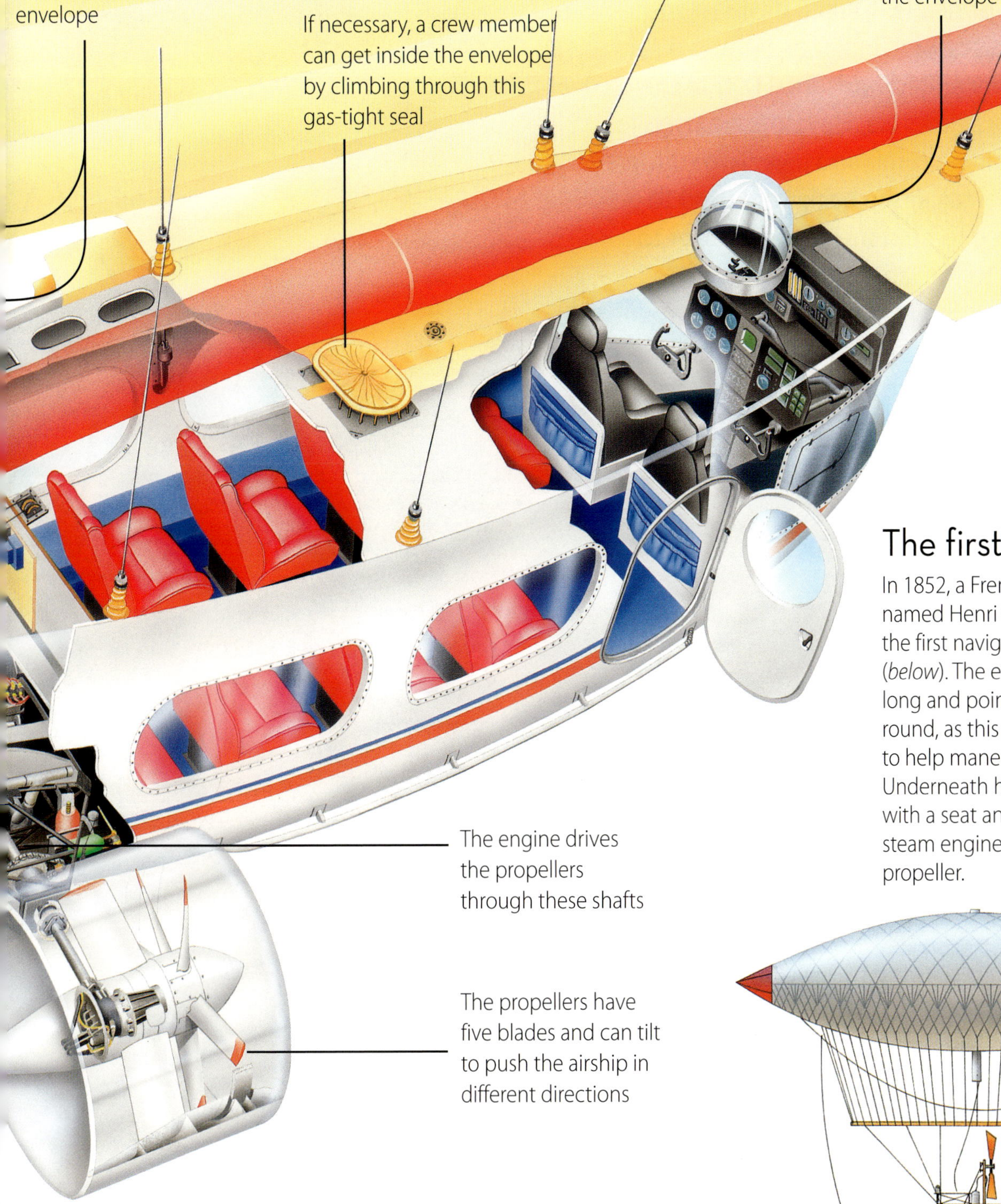

Flying an airship

To descend, more air is pumped into the ballonets to increase the weight of the airship. The rudder and tail fin can be used to turn or tilt the airship.

The first airship

In 1852, a French engineer named Henri Giffard made the first navigable airship (*below*). The envelope was long and pointed instead of round, as this was thought to help maneuverability. Underneath hung a frame with a seat and a small steam engine that drove a propeller.

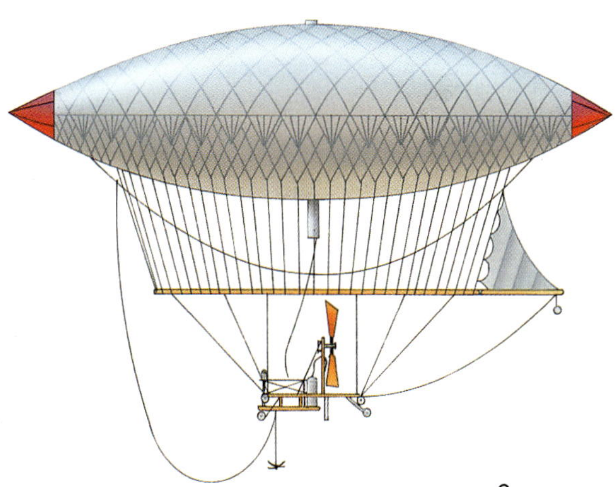

The First Airplane

The first successful powered airplane, called the *Flyer*, was made by American brothers Wilbur and Orville Wright. They began designing and building gliders in the late 1890s. They spent many hours watching birds, noting the way they flew and trying to apply these principles in their designs. The brothers' gliders were biplanes, with two sets of wings. They added horizontal tails at the front to act as elevators. Elevators are used to make an airplane climb and dive. Two rudders in the vertical tail at the back were used to steer the *Flyer*. To hold the wings level, or to roll the *Flyer* to the left or right, wires were added for twisting the wings. Next, they built a 12-horsepower engine and used bicycle chains to turn two big "pusher" propellers. The pilot controlled the *Flyer* with two levers and by shifting his body to the left or right.

Wilbur Wright

Orville Wright

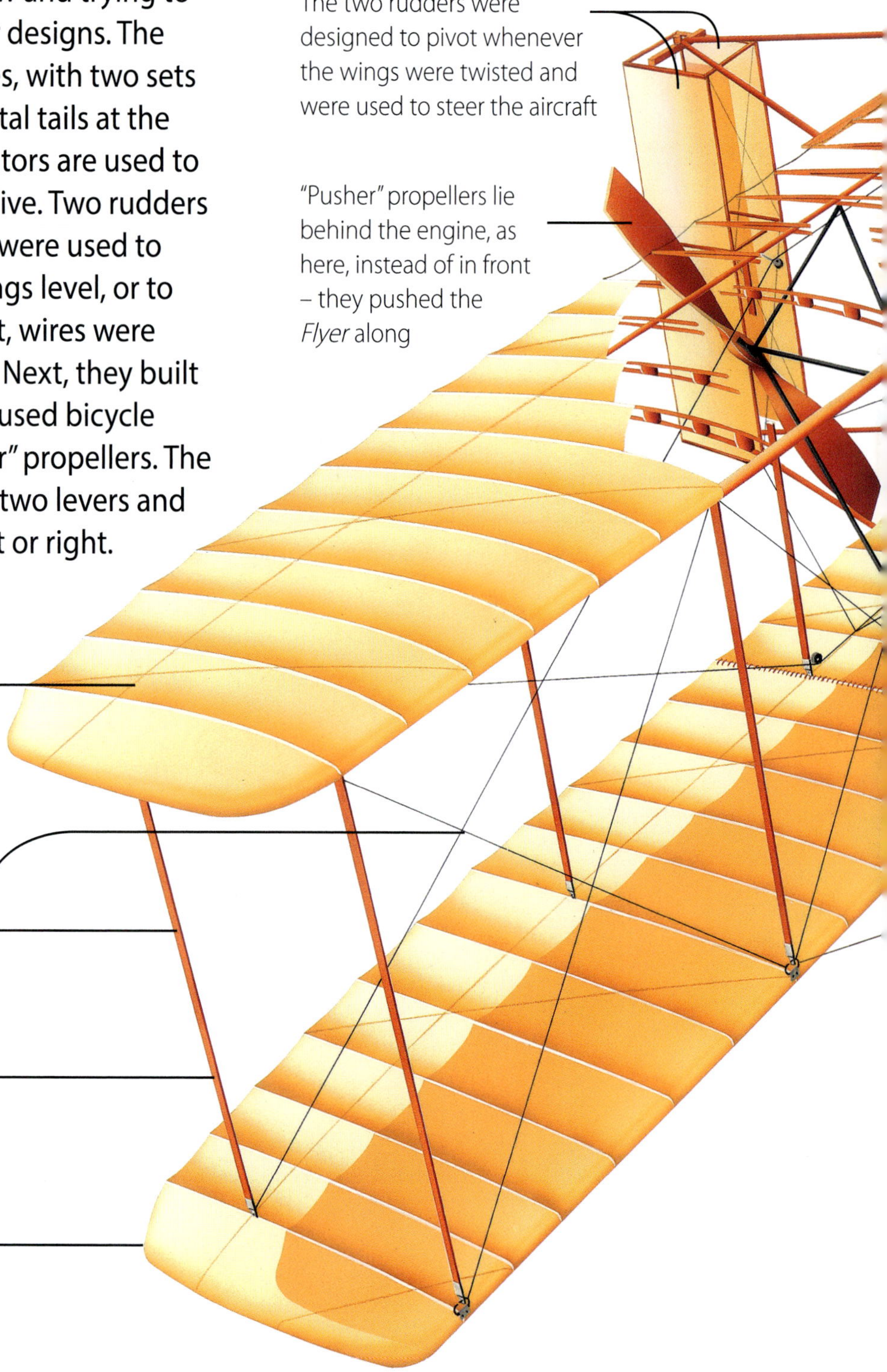

First flight

Orville Wright made the world's first powered airplane flight on December 17, 1903. The above photograph shows him in flight on November 16, 1904, at Huffman Prairie in *Wright Flyer II*, which flew about 1,760 feet (536 m) in 40.2 seconds.

Starship

After the Wright brothers' airplane, few aircraft designers put the horizontal tail at the front. It was 70 years before canard (tail-first) airplanes came back into fashion. Several recent fighters have a front tail, called a foreplane. Even a few business and private aircraft have tested the canard design. The Beech Starship (*right*) first flew in 1986. It was a canard business aircraft, with twin "pusher" turboprop engines and up to nine seats. Only 53 Starships were ever built.

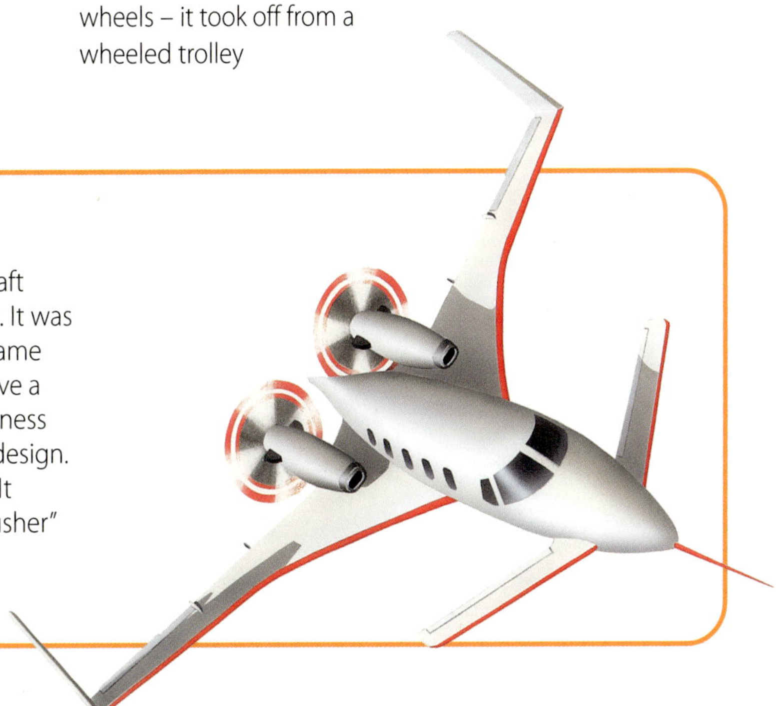

Early Airplanes

Before 1930, most airplanes were made of wood, or steel tubes, or both. They were usually held firm with tensioned wires and covered with flimsy fabric. Designers then began to make airplanes entirely out of metal. A strong metal skin, or outer layer, could withstand the pushes, pulls, and twists of flight. This meant that designers could do away with wires and struts. Next, retractable landing gear was added, so the wheels could be folded away inside the airplane after takeoff.

1915 All-metal aircraft

Apart from an unsuccessful machine of 1910, the Junkers J 1 of December 1915 was the first all-metal aircraft. This German monoplane was made of steel sheets, protected by a thin layer of tin.

Junkers J 1

1939 Jet airplane

First flown on August 27, 1939, the Heinkel He 178 was the first jet airplane in the world. It was powered by a turbojet engine invented by a German engineer Hans von Ohain. An Englishman, Frank Whittle, had patented a design for the same kind of engine nine years earlier, but few people believed that it would work.

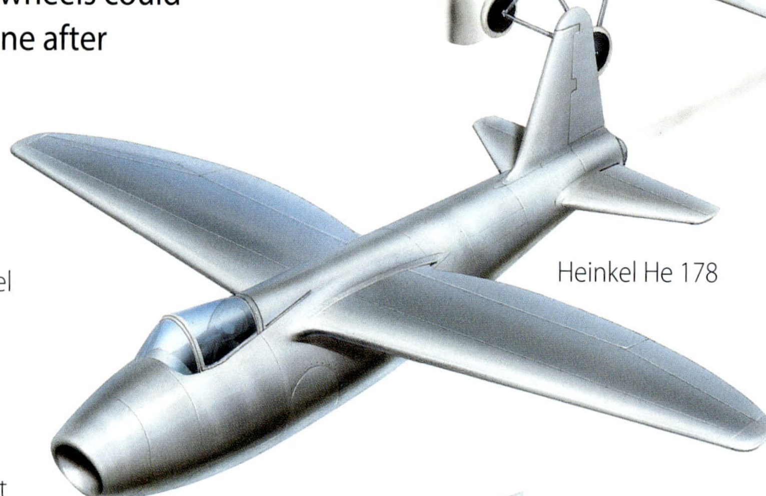

Heinkel He 178

1951 Swept-back wings

Engineers discovered that a fast jet can go even faster if its wings are swept back. The Bell X-5 was first flown in the United States in 1951. Its wings could be pivoted from 20 to 60 degrees during flight.

Bell X-5

1913 Bigger and better

A young engineer from Russia, Igor Sikorsky, built an airplane in 1913 that was far bigger than any built before. The S-21 Russki Vityaz had four engines, glass windows, a carpet, a sofa, and electric light!

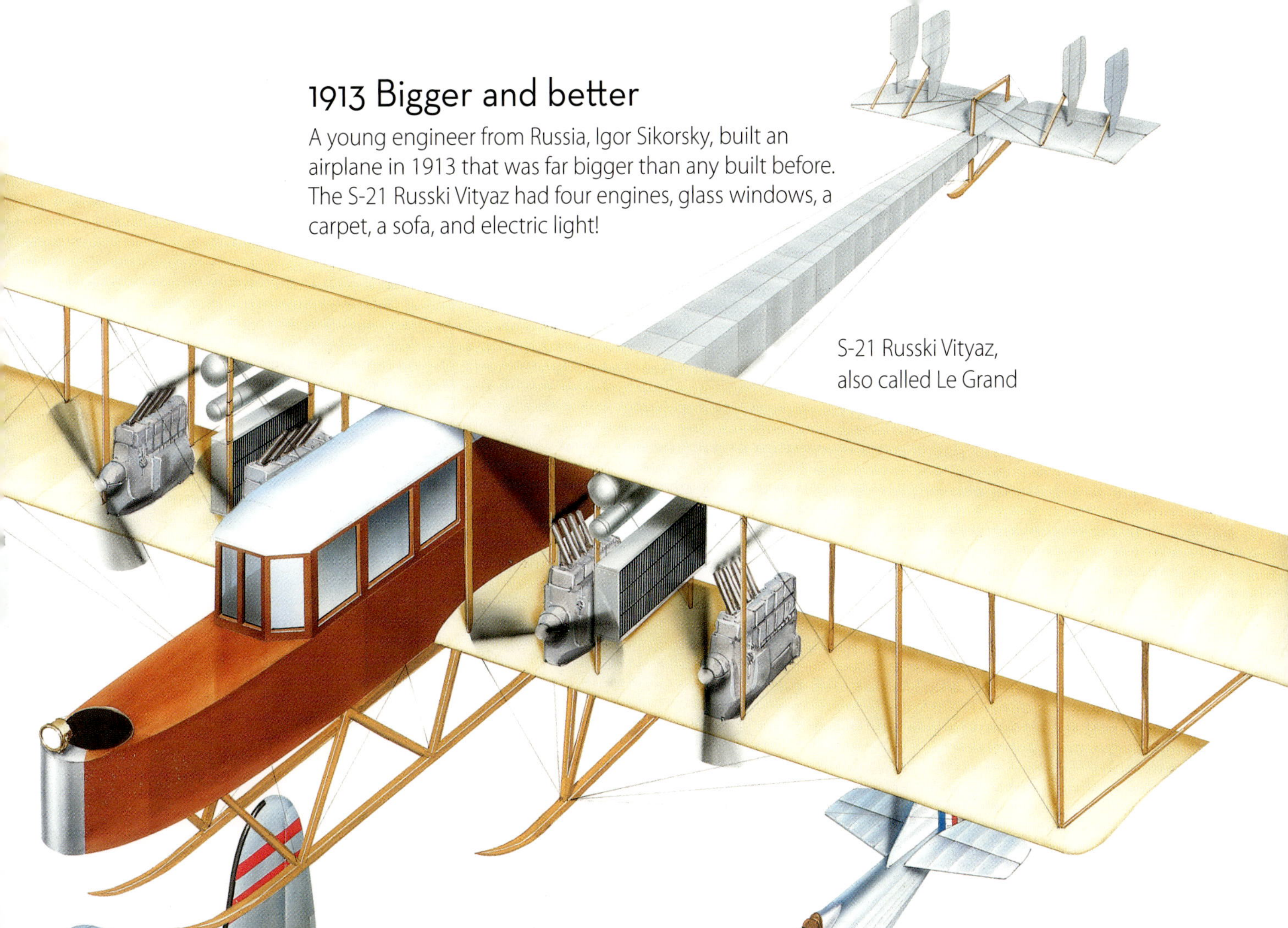

S-21 Russki Vityaz, also called Le Grand

Verville-Sperry R-3

1938 Passenger airliner

Boeing built the first passenger airliner with a pressurized cabin, the 307 Stratoliner. As aircraft climb higher, the air gets thinner. Fresh air was pumped into the Boeing's cabin so the passengers could breathe more easily.

Boeing 307 Stratoliner

Retractable landing gear

The Verville-Sperry R-3 racer was one of the first airplanes to have retractable landing gear, following the Dayton Wright RB-1 of 1920. The Verville-Sperry R-3 had a monoplane wing without wires, and a streamlined body to reduce air resistance.

How Airplanes Fly

For an airplane to fly, it must have one or more wings, a propulsion system (propeller or jet), and flight controls to guide it. To stop an airplane from being pulled down to earth by its own weight, a force called lift must be generated. To do this an airplane must be traveling fast enough and its wings must be a special cambered, or curved, shape (*see right*).

The whole body of an airplane must have a streamlined, or smooth, shape so air can pass freely around it. A shape that is not streamlined would cause greater friction with the air, known as drag, which works against the aircraft's forward motion.

Lift

The upward force caused by a wing moving through the air is called lift. Almost all lift is produced by the air that passes across the more-curved top of the wing. This air has to speed up and rush over the wing much faster than the air passing underneath. Speeding up the air greatly reduces its pressure, so that it sucks the wing upwards.

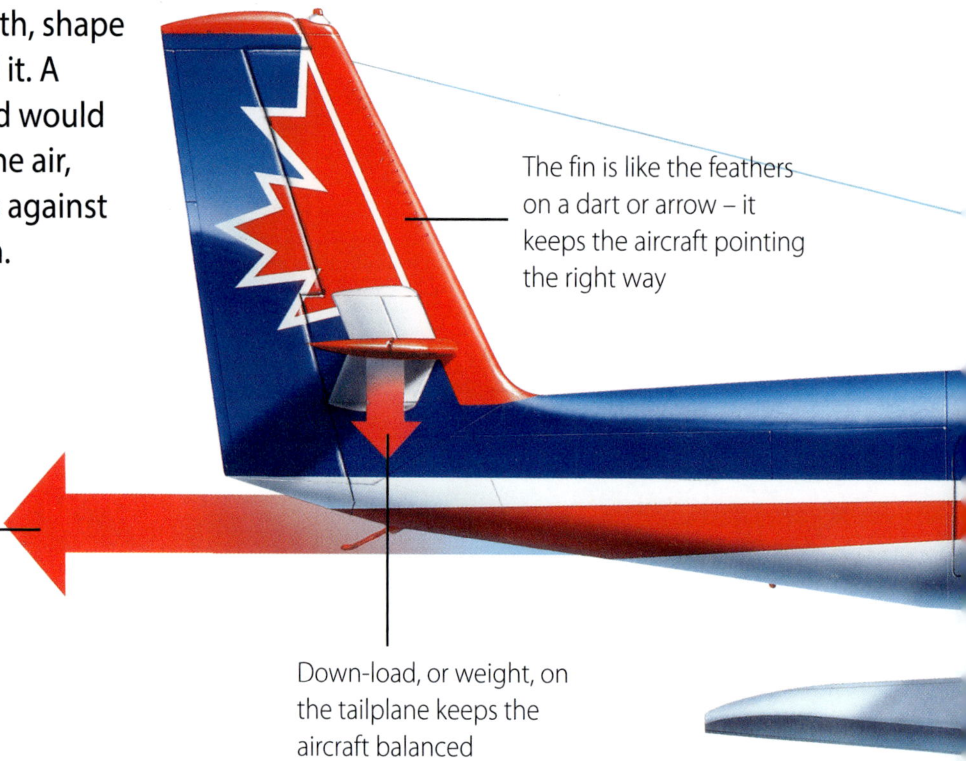

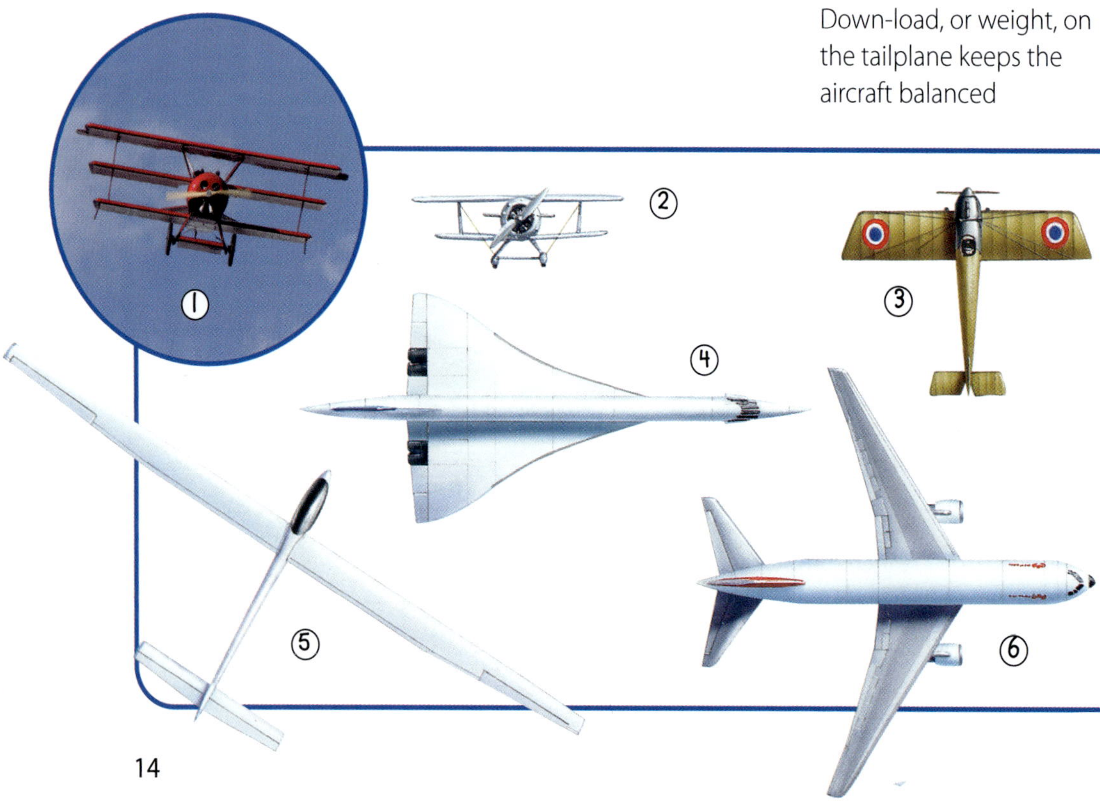

Airplane shapes

(1) A triplane (three sets of wings) fighter of 1917. (2) A biplane (two sets of wings). (3) A monoplane (with one set of wings) fighter of 1915. (4) The distinctive Concorde, a former supersonic airliner. (5) A glider, with long slender wings to help it stay airborne without an engine. (6) A passenger airliner, with two jet engines.

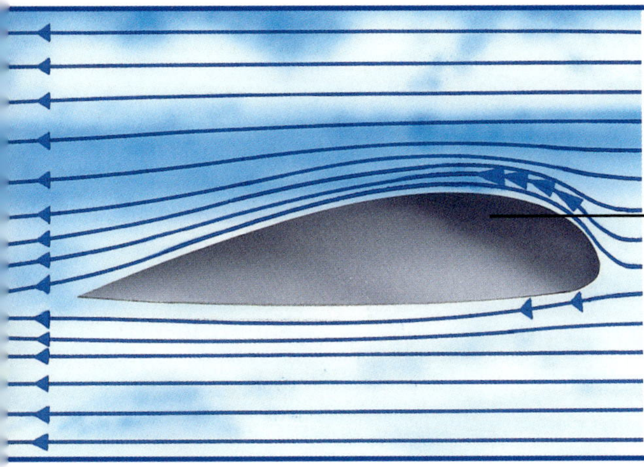

The air rushing over the wing has to travel farther, so it goes faster and has a lower pressure

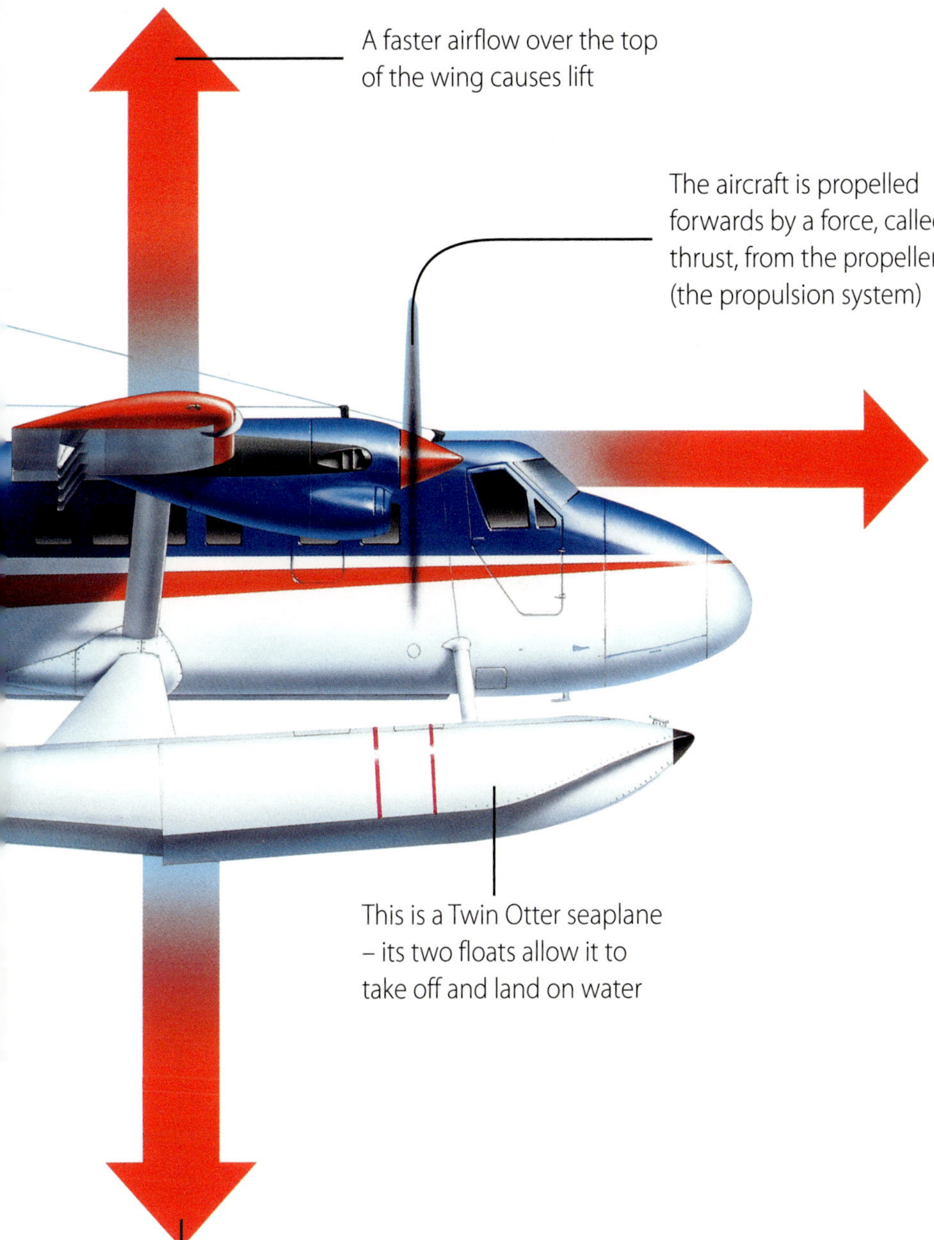

A faster airflow over the top of the wing causes lift

The aircraft is propelled forwards by a force, called thrust, from the propellers (the propulsion system)

This is a Twin Otter seaplane – its two floats allow it to take off and land on water

Without lift, the weight of the aircraft would pull it down to earth

Wings

As aircraft technology has developed, the shape of the wing in cross-section, called the aerofoil, has changed.

Early aviation pioneers used wings which were just flat sheets, set at an angle.

The Wright brothers made their wings cambered (curved) to generate more lift.

In World War II, heavy bombers had thick metal wings, which were able to lift well at low speeds.

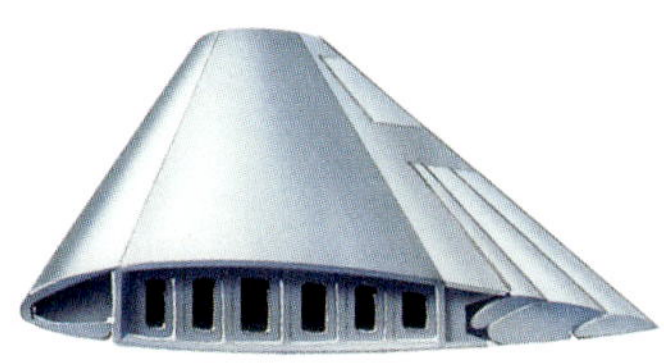

Early jet airliners had thinner wings, with slats and powerful flaps.

Some aircraft have "super-critical" wings that are flatter on top and bulged underneath, which improves performance at both very high and low speeds.

The Controls

Inside the Boeing 747, or "Jumbo Jet," there are more than 5,000 sets of control mechanisms. Pilots control the airplane with the help of a system of hinged parts, called control surfaces. These control surfaces are moved by powerful hydraulic jacks. From the cockpit, the pilot sends commands through a mechanical system of cables to make the hydraulic jacks push, pull, and rotate the surfaces.

The control surfaces include: ailerons (for roll); elevators (for climb and dive); rudder (for direction); spoilers (for roll, and to act as airbrakes); and leading-edge slats and trailing-edge flaps (to give extra lift at low speeds, such as when the airplane is landing).

The cockpit

Most transport aircraft, such as this Boeing 747, have a cockpit that seats two pilots (*see below right*). Each pilot has a set of controls. A control column is turned to roll the aircraft, or is pushed or pulled to make it dive or climb, and there are pedals to operate the rudder.

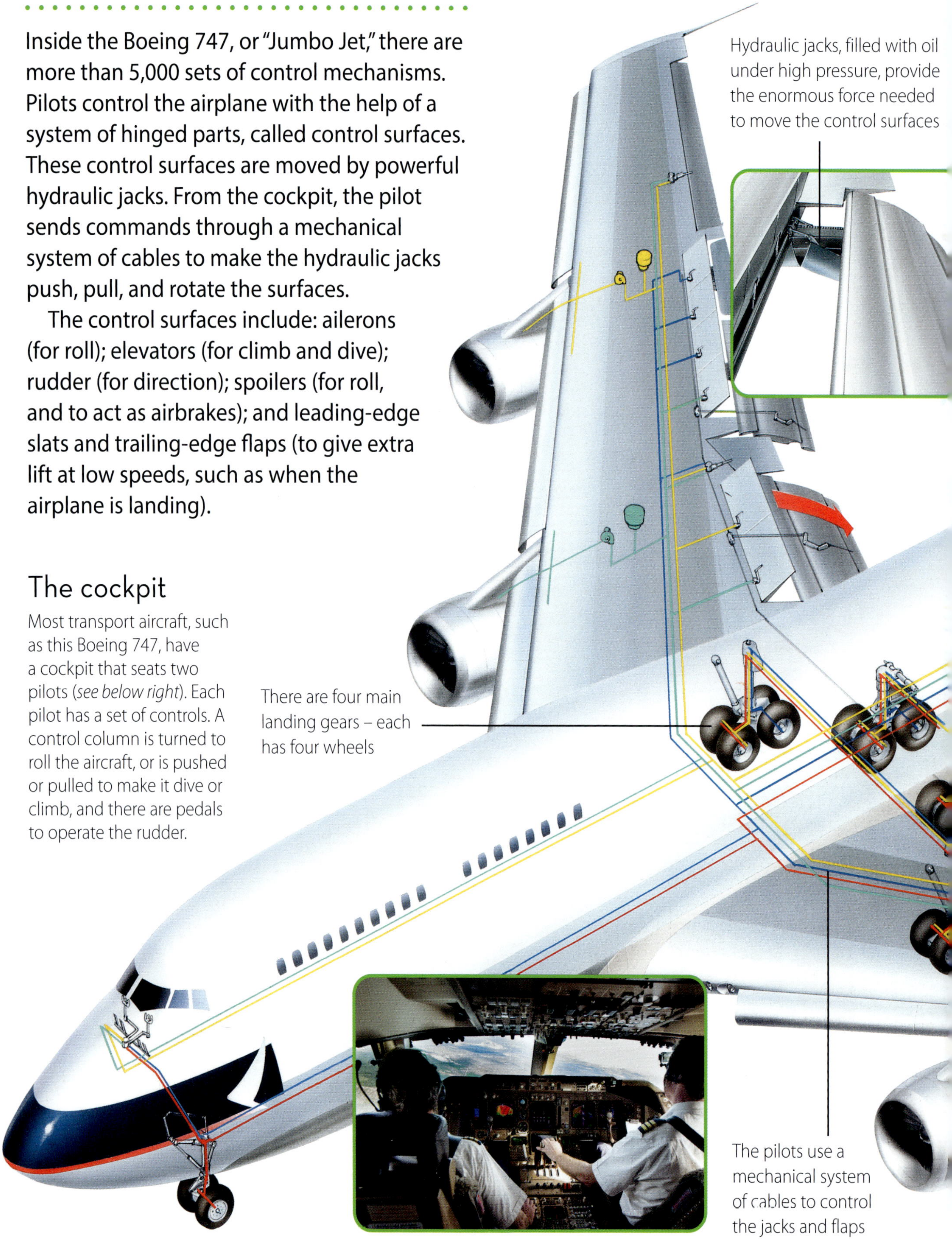

Hydraulic jacks, filled with oil under high pressure, provide the enormous force needed to move the control surfaces

The pilots use a mechanical system of cables to control the jacks and flaps

Flying controls

Rolling (1) is done with ailerons and spoilers. Yawing – turning the nose left or right – is done with the rudder (2). To dive (3), the elevators are moved down. The elevators are moved up to make the aircraft climb (4).

Fly-by-wire

The Airbus A320 (*left*) was designed after the Boeing 747, and instead of having mechanical connections, it uses fly-by-wire. The pilots' commands are sent as electrical signals along wires. The pilots use joysticks (*below*) connected to five computers. The tail has backup mechanical controls, but the chance of a complete fly-by-wire failure is 1 in 1,000,000,000.

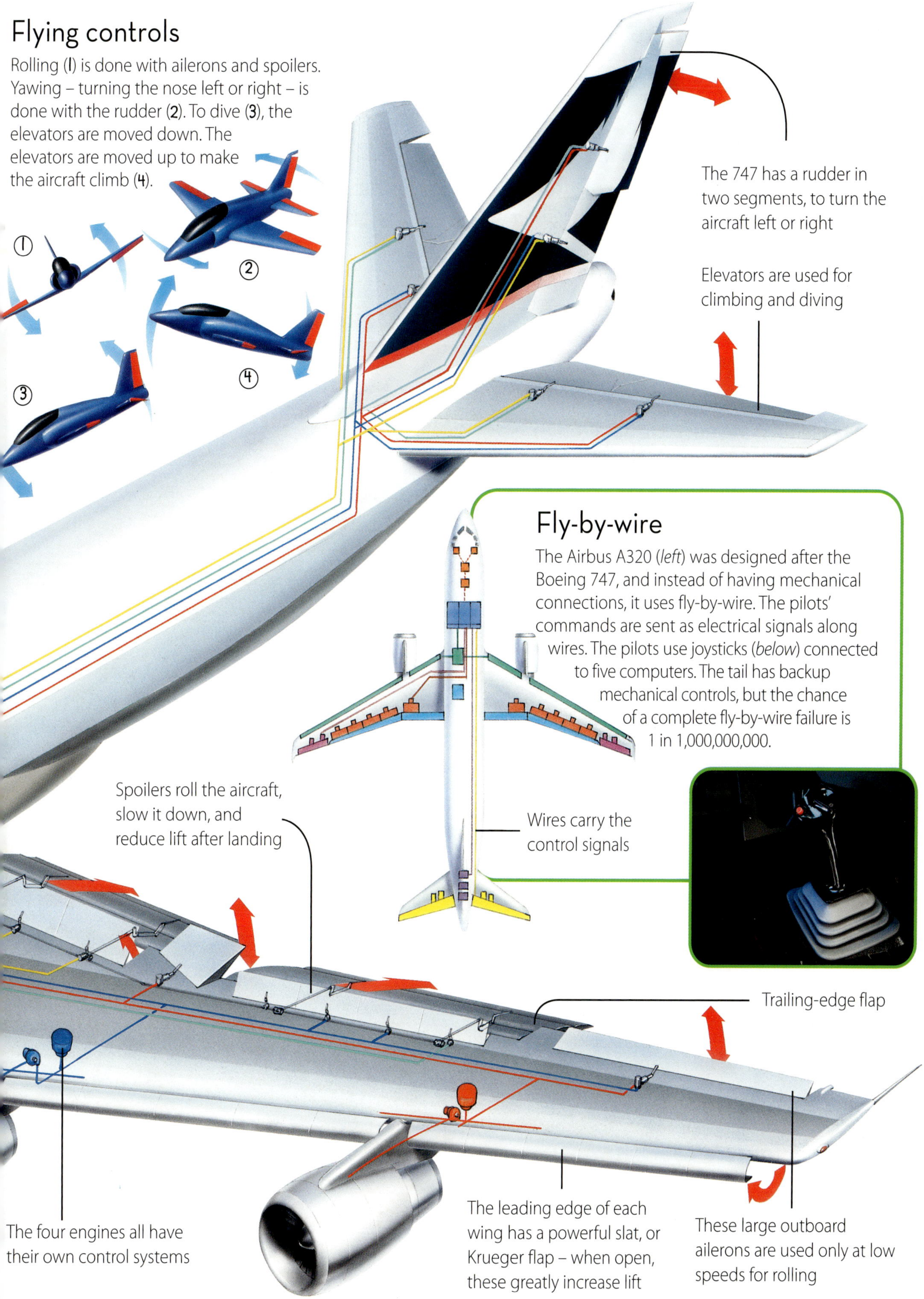

Control Surfaces

The wing of a typical jet airliner changes shape before and after takeoff, and before and after landing. To gain more lift on takeoff, the pilot extends huge flaps along the back (trailing edge) of the wing. Before landing, the pilot extends the flaps further, to increase lift even more as the aircraft slows down. On landing, spoilers are immediately raised to reduce lift and keep the aircraft down on the runway.

Small ailerons are raised or lowered to control the roll of the aircraft. Rolling or banking is necessary for turning. Further out along the wing are bigger ailerons, used only at low speeds. Along the front of the wing (leading edge) are slats or flaps which can also increase lift at low speeds.

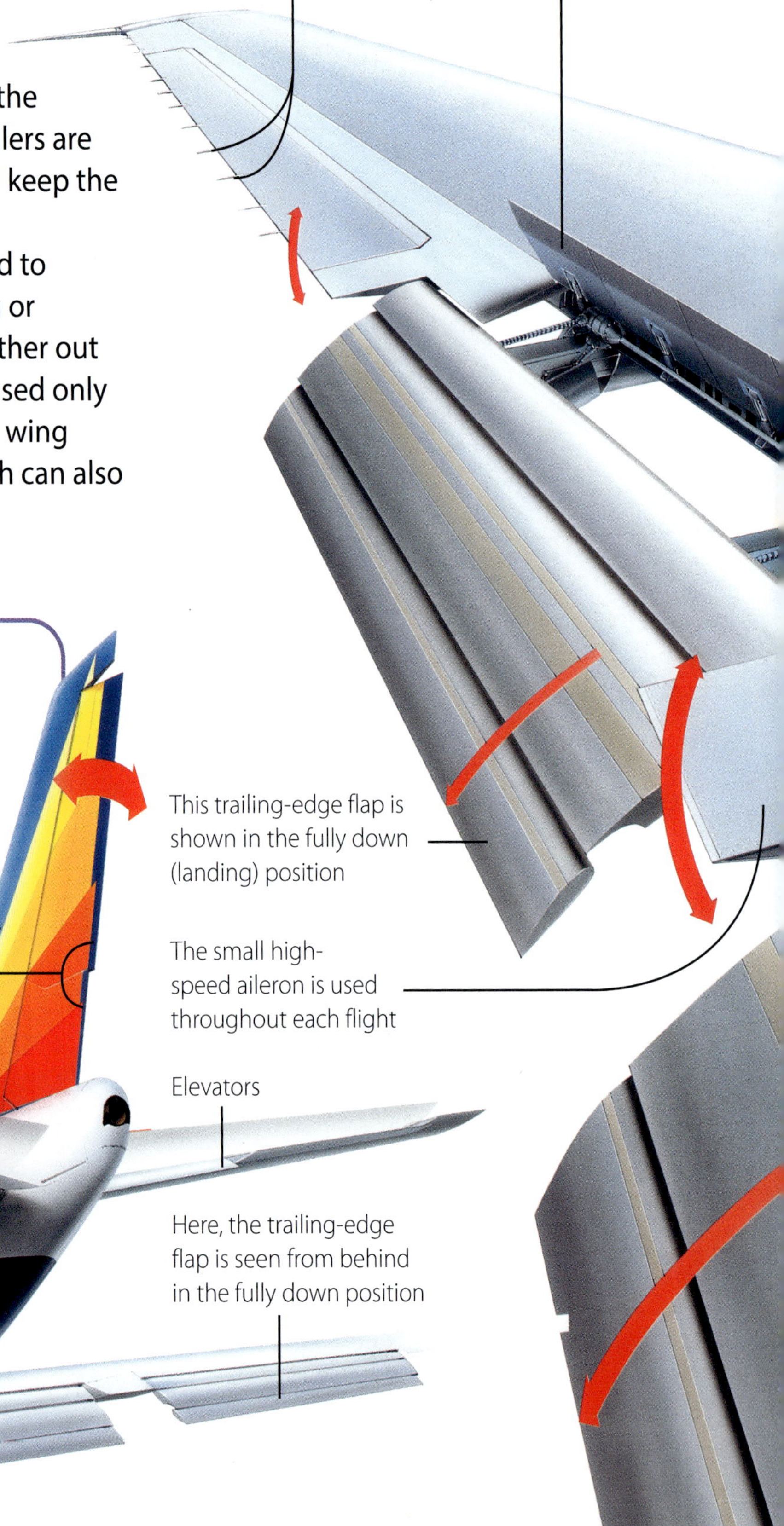

Fin and tailplane

An airplane's tail usually has a fin and a tailplane. A rudder is attached to the fin. Pivoted elevators are attached to the tailplane. In a multiengined jet the rudder is not used much, except in crosswind landings, or if an engine fails.

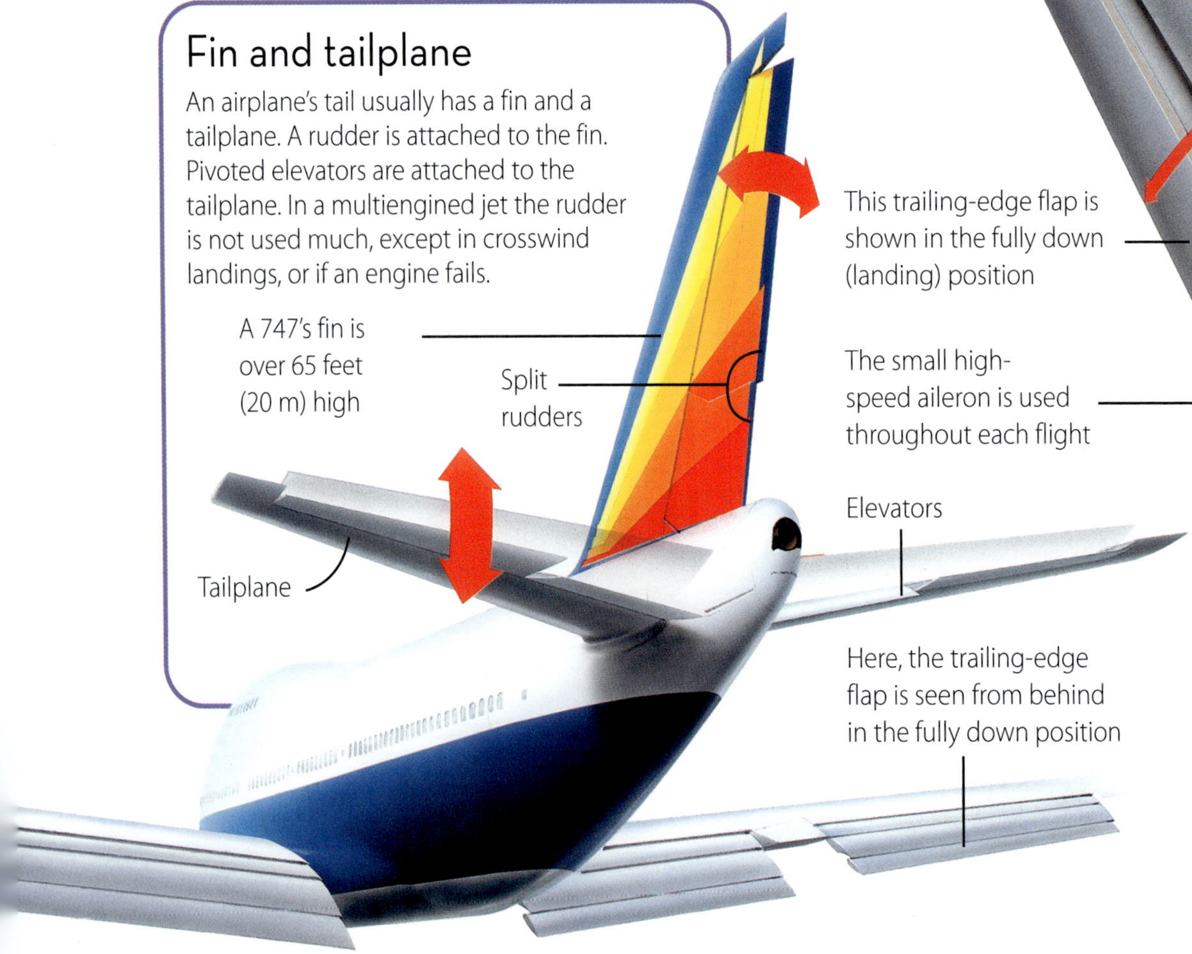

Flaps and spoilers

When a wing changes shape, the airflow is affected and the speed and direction of the aircraft is altered. Trailing-edge flaps can be lowered to increase drag and slow the aircraft down (*below left*). The leading-edge flaps are extended to give the extra lift needed at a low speed. When spoilers are raised (*below right*), the airflow pushes the wing down, creating even more drag and reducing lift.

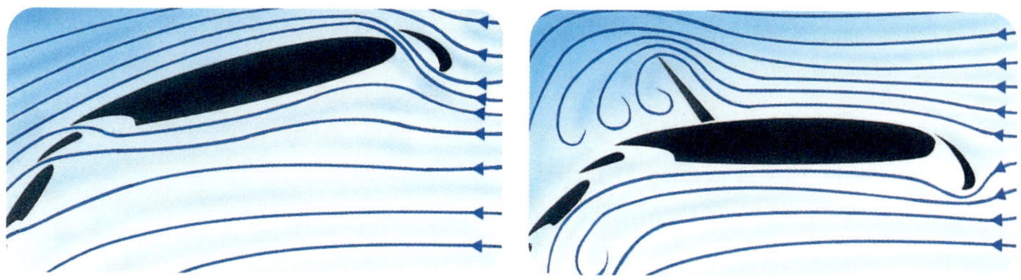

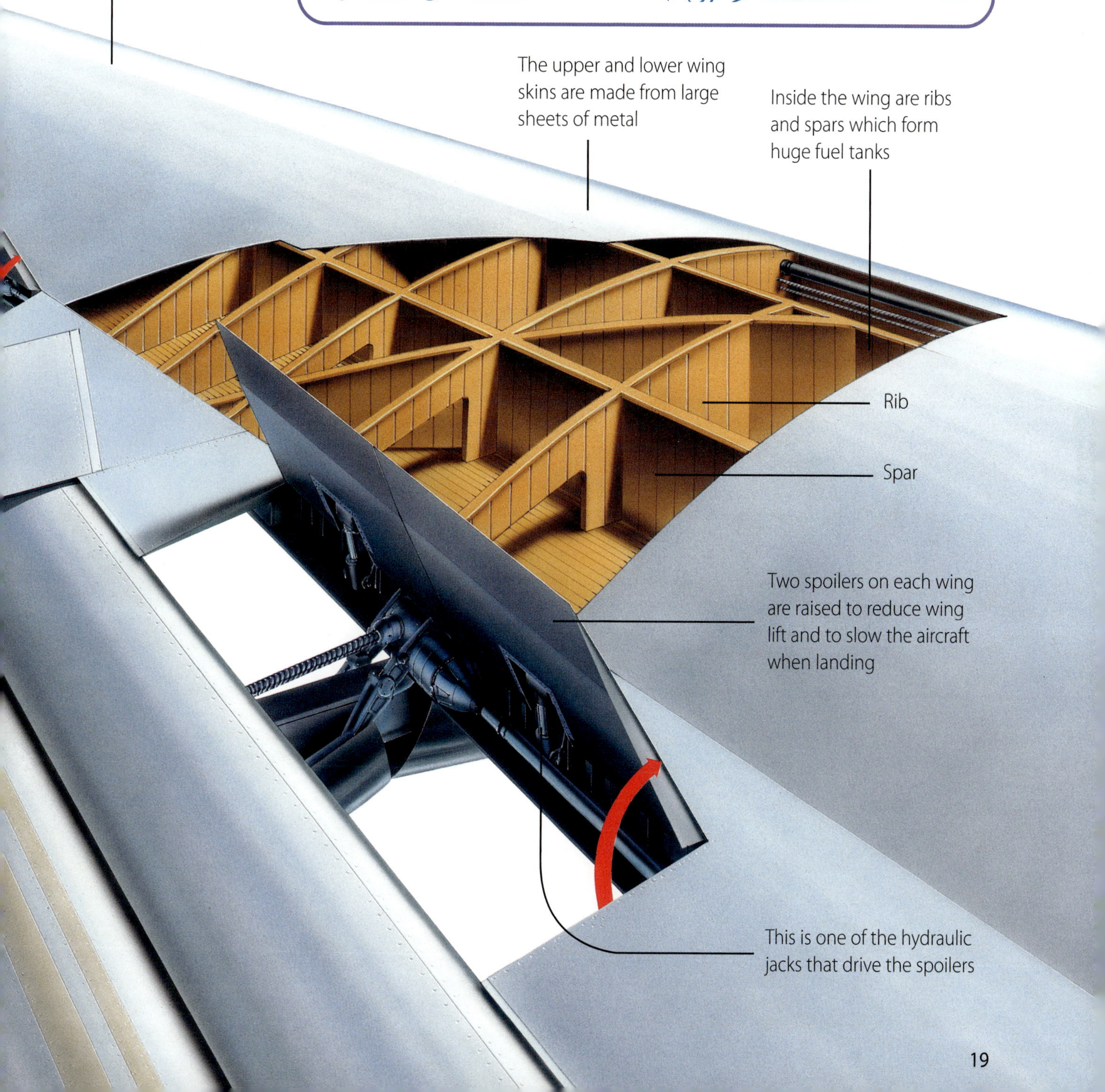

Inside the Cockpit

Early cockpits had very few instruments, but as aircraft developed and improved, it become more difficult for pilots of large airplanes to manage all of the aircraft's systems. Then came a revolutionary new cockpit (*right*). The cockpit in the Airbus 340, which first flew in 1991, has six large color monitors on which the captain (sitting on the left) and the copilot (on the right) can see all the information they need. Overhead are controls for the fuel, hydraulics, electrical systems, cabin pressurization, and air-conditioning, as well as de-icing, emergency oxygen, and other systems. The flight crew contols speed and direction with pedals and a sidestick held in one hand. Under the side windows are the nosewheel tillers for steering the Airbus on the ground. Below the windscreens are controls for the autopilot, which can keep the airplane on a course set by the pilots.

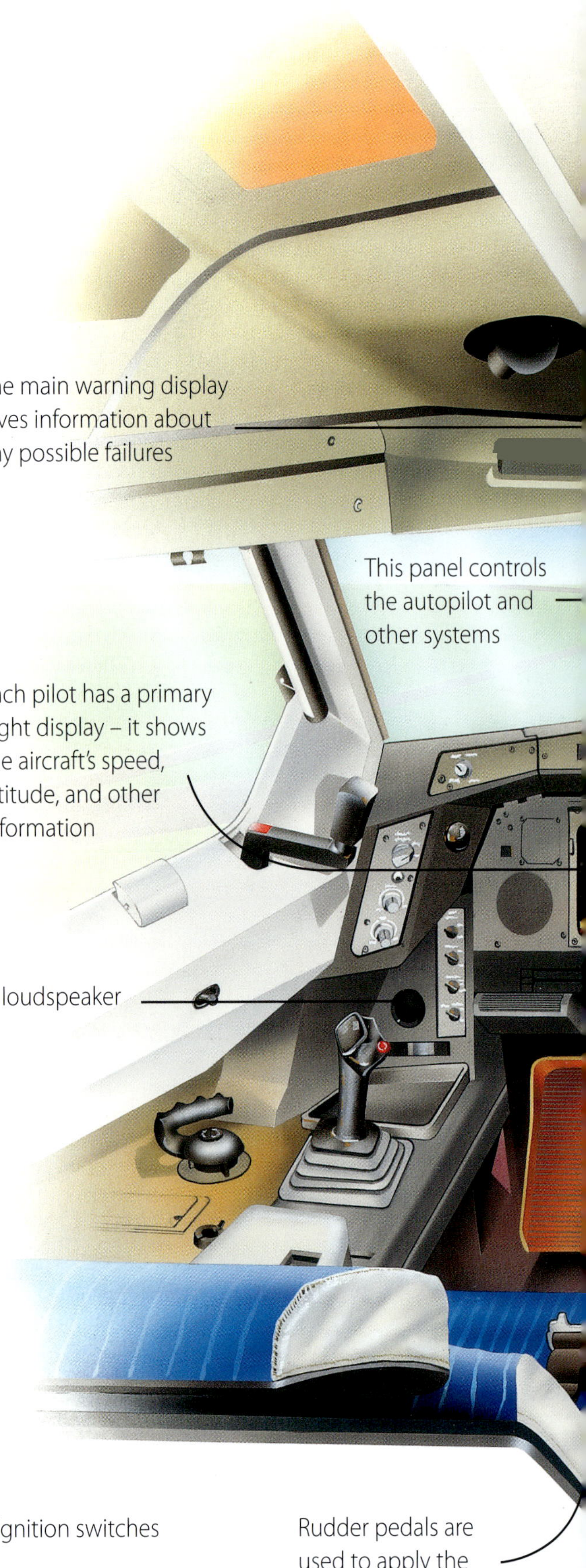

Early cockpit

This is a cockpit from a 1930s biplane. There are just a few essential instruments. Two ignition switches are turned on before starting the engine. A compass for navigation is set into the bottom of the panel.

The overhead panel controls systems which require less monitoring, such as engine-starting, cabin pressurization, and de-icing
A navigation display shows the aircraft's location and what the weather is like ahead
A nosewheel tiller used to steer the plan when it is on the ground
When flying manually (not using the autopilot), the pilot controls the aircraft with this sidestick
Small levers control the flaps, spoilers, and landing gear
These four big levers are the throttles, which control the power of the engines
One of three multipurpose control and display units on the central console

Parts of an Airplane

Very few airplanes, such as the U.S. Air Force B-2 Spirit "stealth bomber," are just flying wings, without a body. Most have a body, called the fuselage, and a tail. The tail usually consists of a fixed vertical fin, to which the rudder is hinged, and fixed tailplanes, to which the elevators are hinged.

The most successful jet fighter of recent times, the F-16 Fighting Falcon (*right and bottom right*) has one-piece pivoting tailplanes. These are used instead of elevators, for climbing and diving. The F-16's fuselage is packed with electronics, fuel, and the engine with its air duct. The pilot sits, or almost lies, in a sloping ejection seat at the front. There is a perfect all-round view through the canopy. The F-16 first flew in 1971 and almost 4,000 are in service. It is no longer made for the U.S. Air Force, but F-16s are still built for other countries.

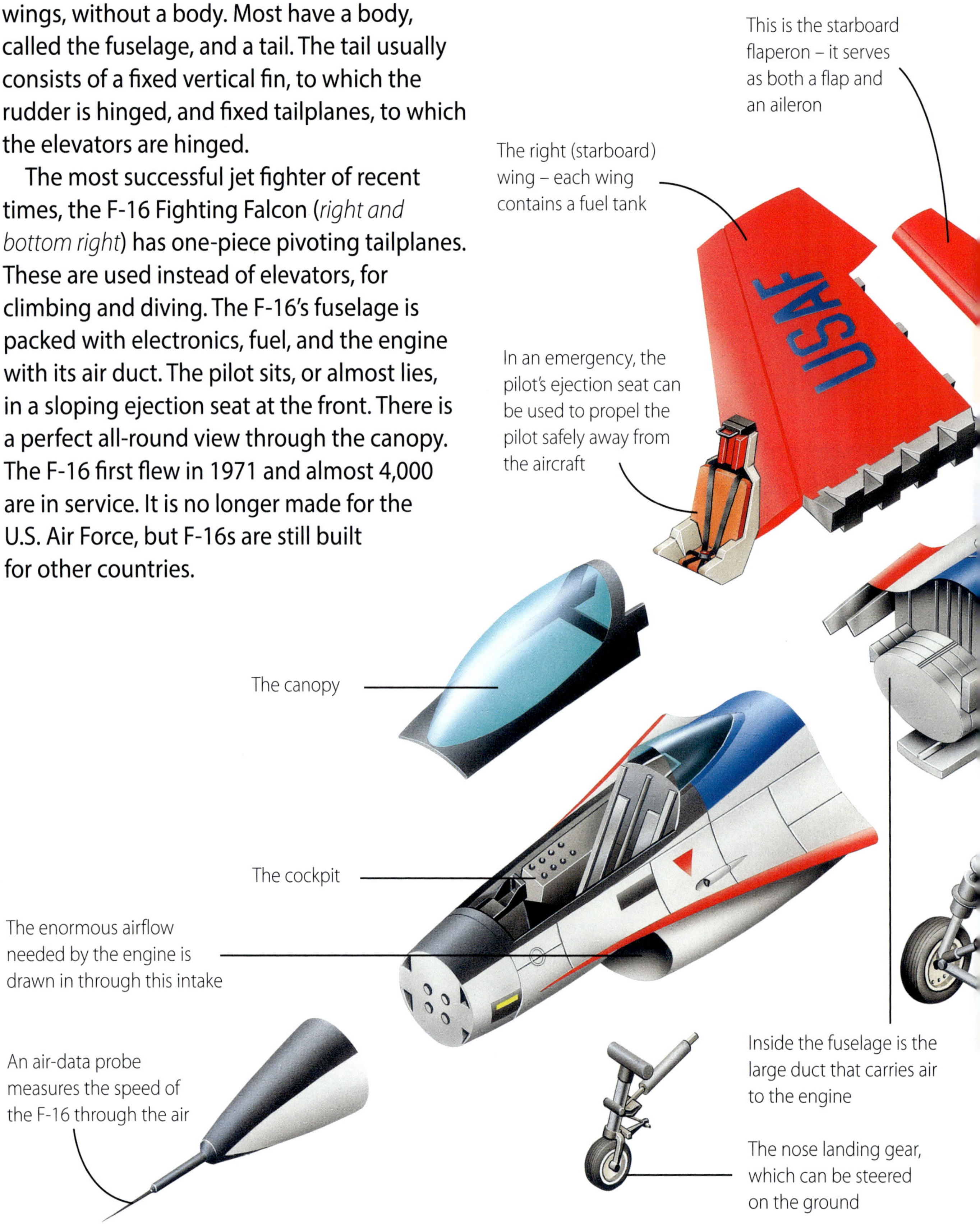

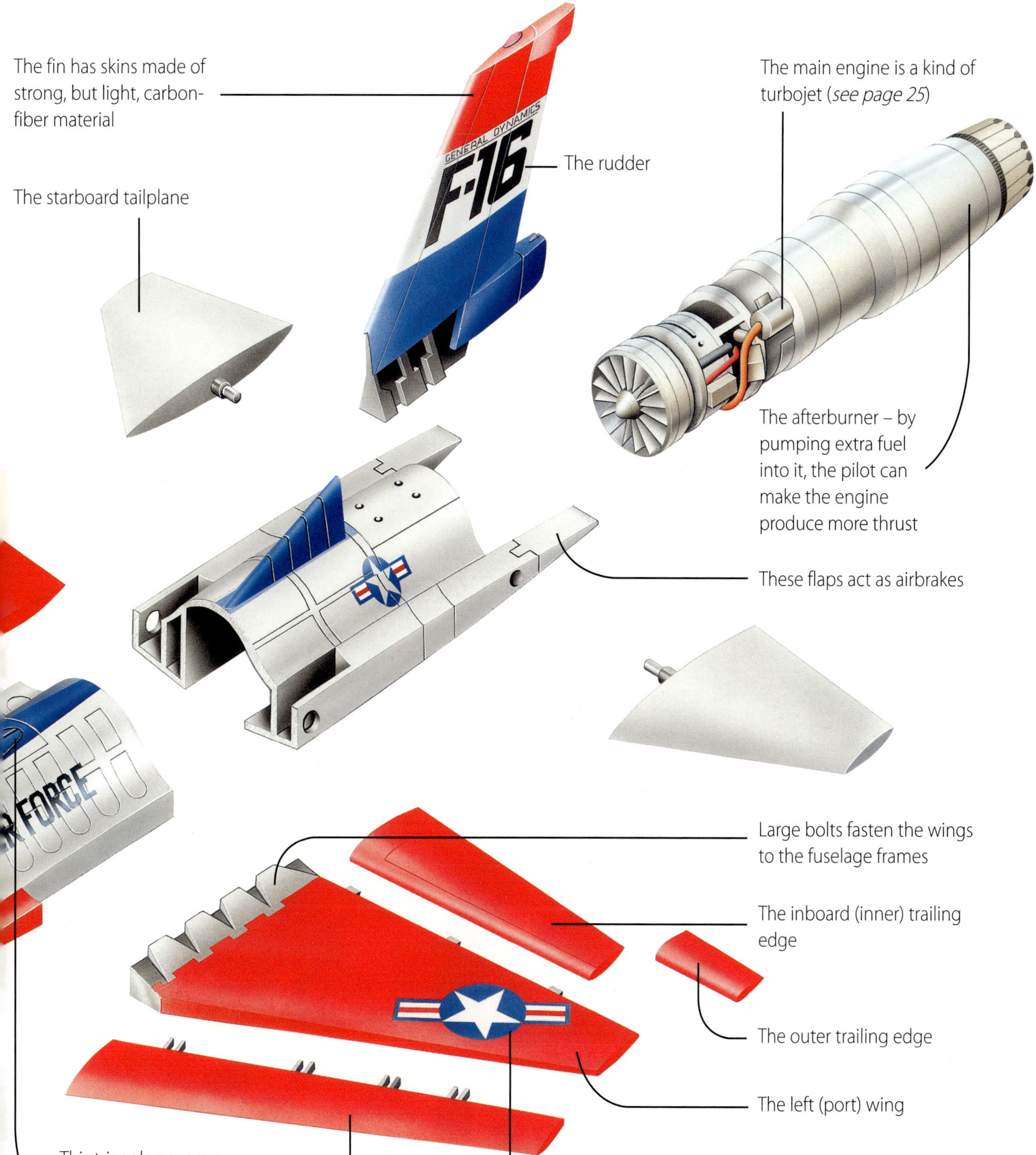

The fin has skins made of strong, but light, carbon-fiber material
GENERAL DYNAMICS
F-16
The rudder
The main engine is a kind of turbojet (*see page 25*)
The starboard tailplane
The afterburner – by pumping extra fuel into it, the pilot can make the engine produce more thrust
These flaps act as airbrakes
Large bolts fasten the wings to the fuselage frames
The inboard (inner) trailing edge
The outer trailing edge
The left (port) wing
This triangle covers a socket for taking on fuel in midair refueling
The leading-edge flap
Each main wing has eight spars inside running from end to end for extra strength
The main landing gears, each with a single wheel

Engine Power

The first powered aircraft, such as the *Flyer* (*see page 10*), used propellers which pushed them along. A propeller draws air in at the front and throws it backwards. This thrusts the propeller and aircraft forwards. The jet of air thrown back by the propellers does not travel very fast, so the maximum speed of a propeller-powered aircraft is about 500 miles per hour (800 kph). Faster speeds can only be achieved by using a different type of engine. Today, the fastest aircraft use turbojet or turbofan engines instead of propellers.

Piston engines

On smaller aircraft, propellers are usually driven by a piston engine, which is similar to a car engine. A Continental O-240A piston engine is shown below. Made by Rolls-Royce, it weighed 247 pounds (112 kg) and produced 130 horsepower. Inside the engine are four cylinders which each contain a piston. Fuel and air are burned to drive the pistons, which push the crankshaft around. The rotating crankshaft turns the propeller.

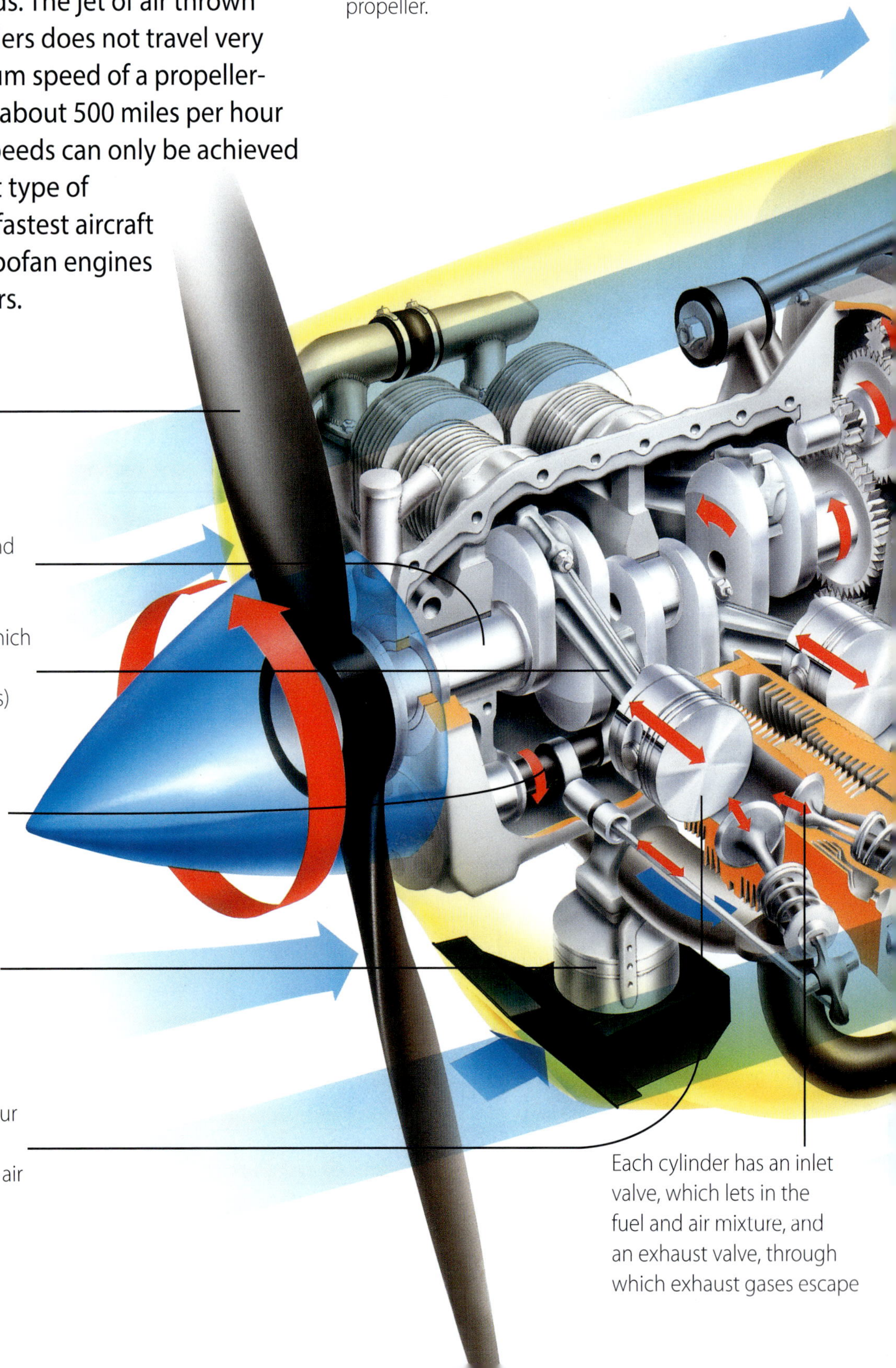

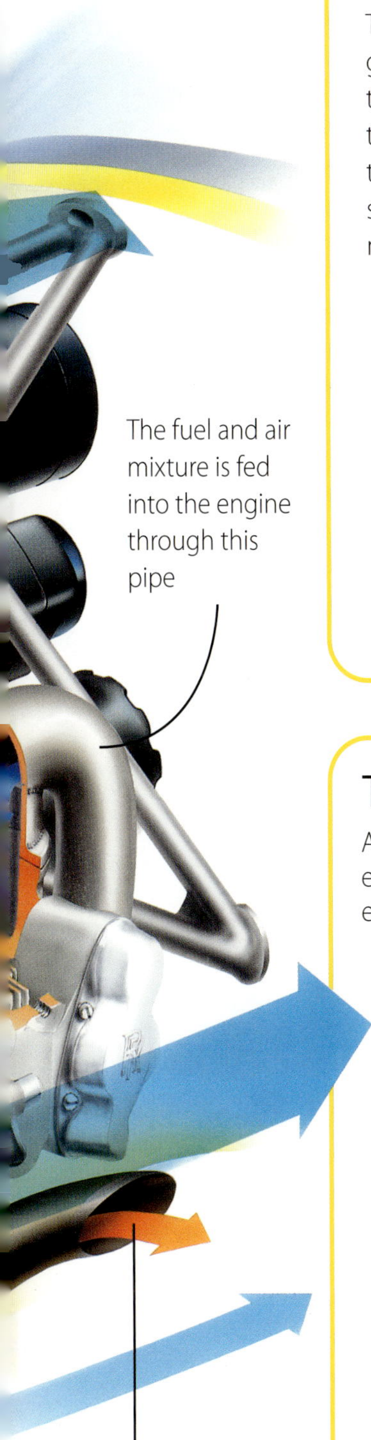

Turboprops

Some propellers are driven by a gas turbine engine, called a turboprop. Because these engines generate more power, some turboprop planes can reach speeds of more than 560 miles per hour (900 kph). The main shaft in a turboprop has to be slowed down, using gears like those in a car (propellers waste power and make too much noise if they spin too fast). Many small airliners, carrying 50–70 passengers, are powered by two turboprops.

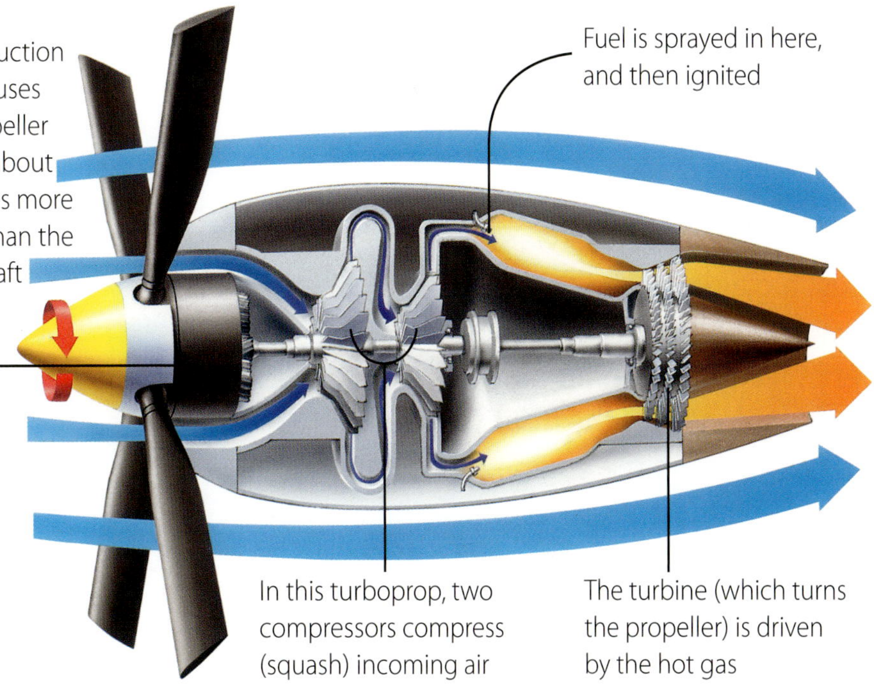

Turbojets

A more powerful gas turbine, the turbojet, was developed in 1937. Aircraft driven by turbojet engines do not have propellers. They are propelled by a backward jet of hot gas. These engines, usually in the form of turbofans (*see page 26*), propel the fastest larger aircraft.

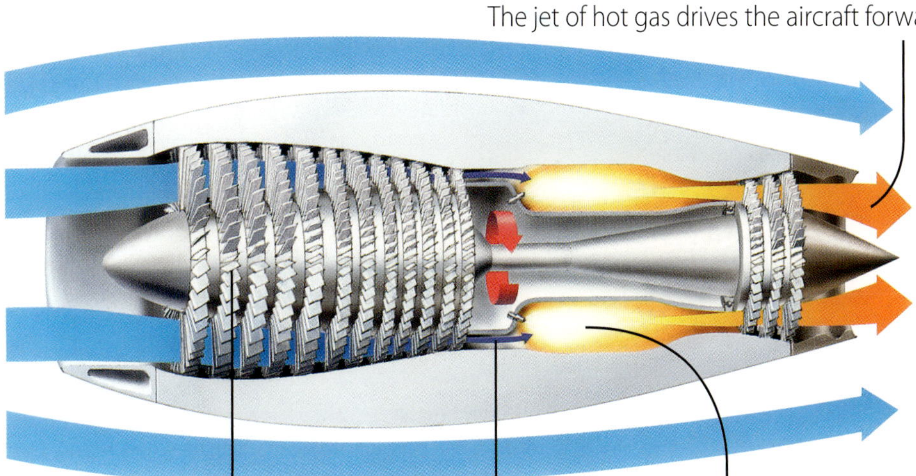

Jet Propulsion

A jet engine drives an aircraft forward with enormous force. Air is sucked in at the front, compressed by blades, and then mixed with fuel. This mixtures ignites, or burns, within the combustion chamber. The air is then expelled at a high speed from the back. This stream of hot air – the "jet" – causes a thrust in the opposite direction (*see below*), propelling the aircraft forwards.

Most big airliners are powered by turbofan engines, which are quieter than other types of jet engines. Air is drawn in by a huge fan spinning at the front. Some of the air passes through the engine, while most flows around the outside, to thrust the aircraft forward. The fan and compressor blades are themselves driven by turbines turned by the stream of hot air rushing out through the back of the engine.

Propulsion

Jet engines work on the principle of jet propulsion. An aircraft is thrust forwards because of a reaction to high-speed air traveling backwards. The same effect can be seen when you let go of the neck of a blown-up balloon. While the neck is pinched, the air pressure inside is the same in all directions, so the balloon remains still. Because the air is compressed inside, when you release the neck of the balloon the air will rush out at high speed. The air pressure at the opposite end to the neck is no longer counterbalanced, so the balloon flies forwards.

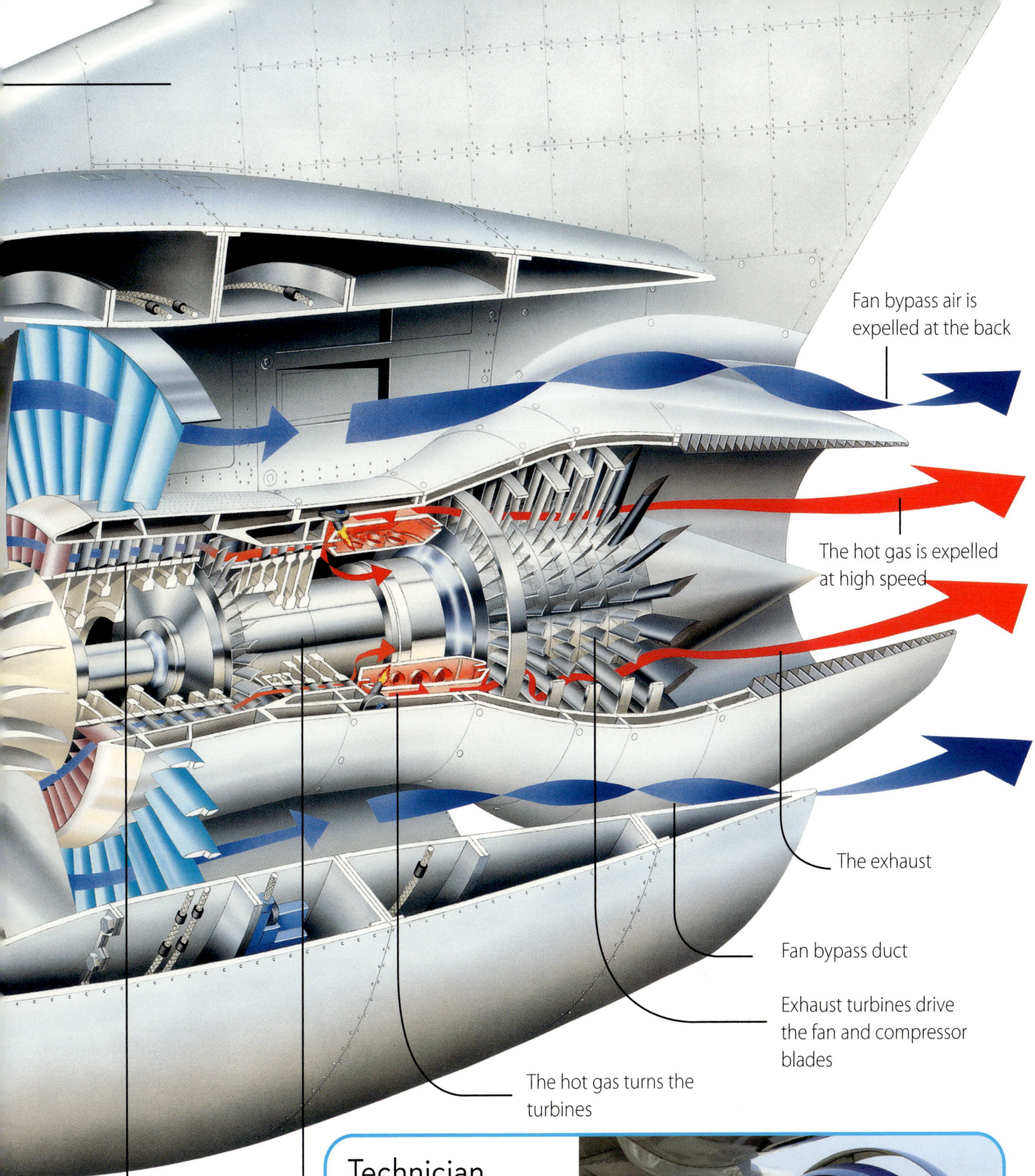

Technician

Just like cars, airplanes have routine checks and maintenance carried out regularly by specialist technicians. Most commerical airplanes have thorough maintenance checks and repairs after approximately every 400 flight hours of the aircraft.

Power Systems

Like most large aircraft, the Boeing 747-400 is controlled by the flight crew via powerful electrical and hydraulic systems. All of the power needed to run these systems comes from fuel, carried in enormous tanks in the wings. The aircraft's four main engines burn fuel for flight, and also drive electric generators, producing around 75 kilowatts each. Two even more powerful electric generators are driven by the APU (*see above right*). Each engine also drives a hydraulic pump. Another four pumps are driven by high-pressure air; these pump hydraulic fluid to move the landing gear, flaps, flight controls, brakes, and other systems. In the belly of the aircraft are the cabin pressurization and air-conditioning systems. When the aircraft is in flight at high altitude, the air outside is too cold and too thin to breathe, so air for the cabin must be pressurized and kept warm.

APU

Most large passenger aircraft have an APU (auxiliary power unit). On the 747 it is at the tip of the tail end of the fuselage. It is a small gas turbine engine, like a miniature jet engine, which drives two electric generators. It also supplies compressed air for starting the main engines and for air-conditioning the cabin. The arrows (*right*) show where air is sucked in and hot exhaust pushed out.

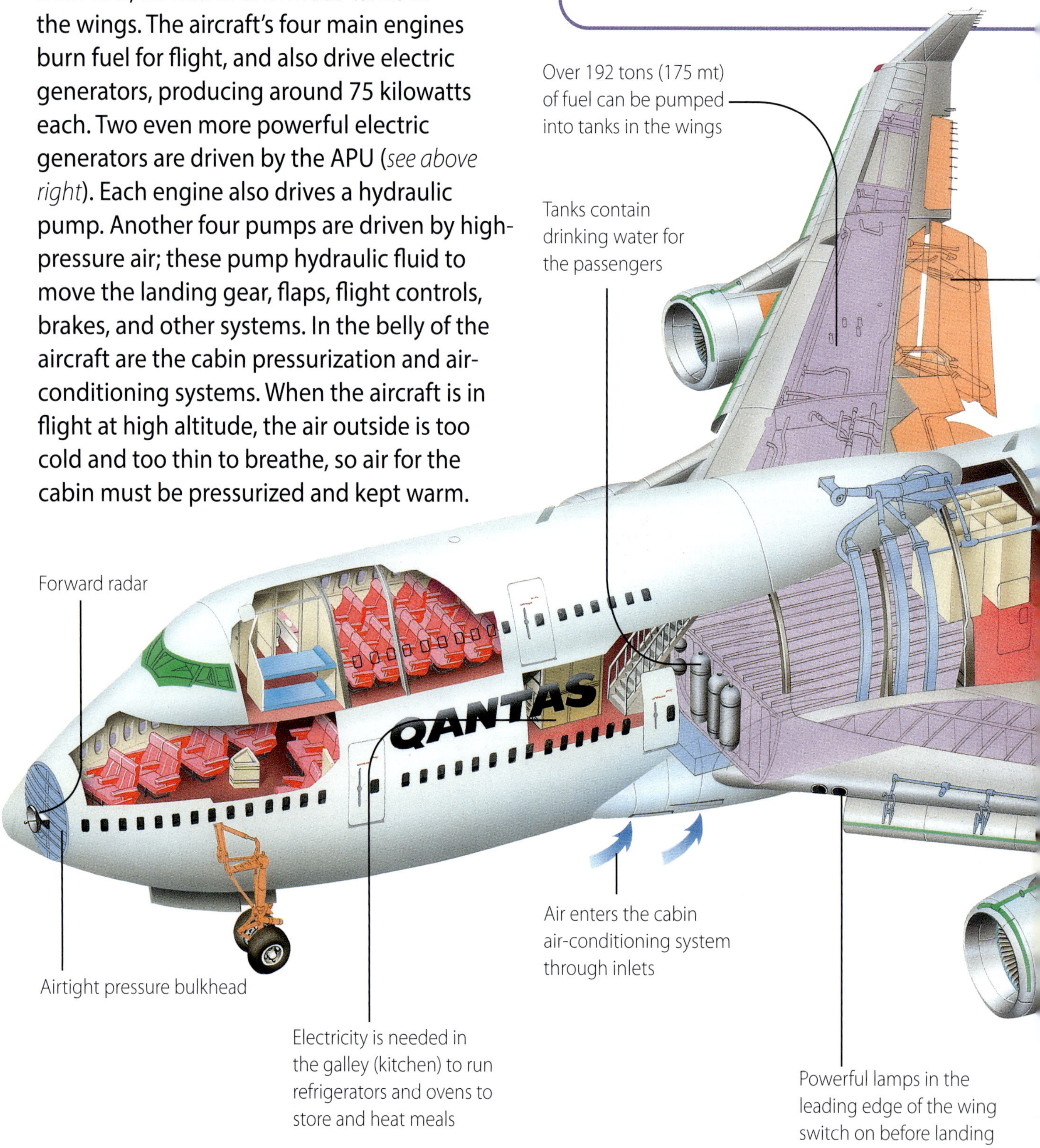

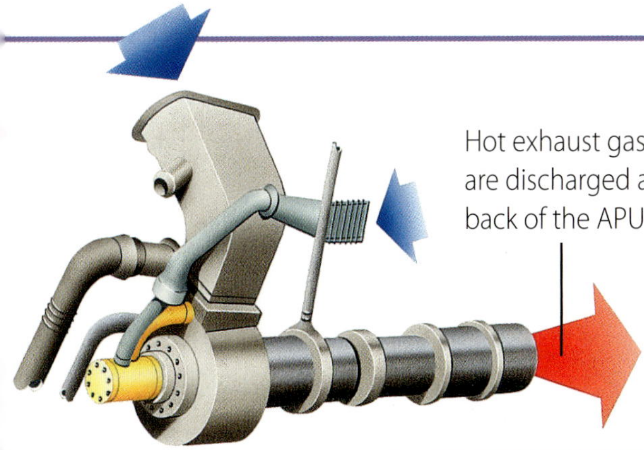
Hot exhaust gases are discharged at the back of the APU

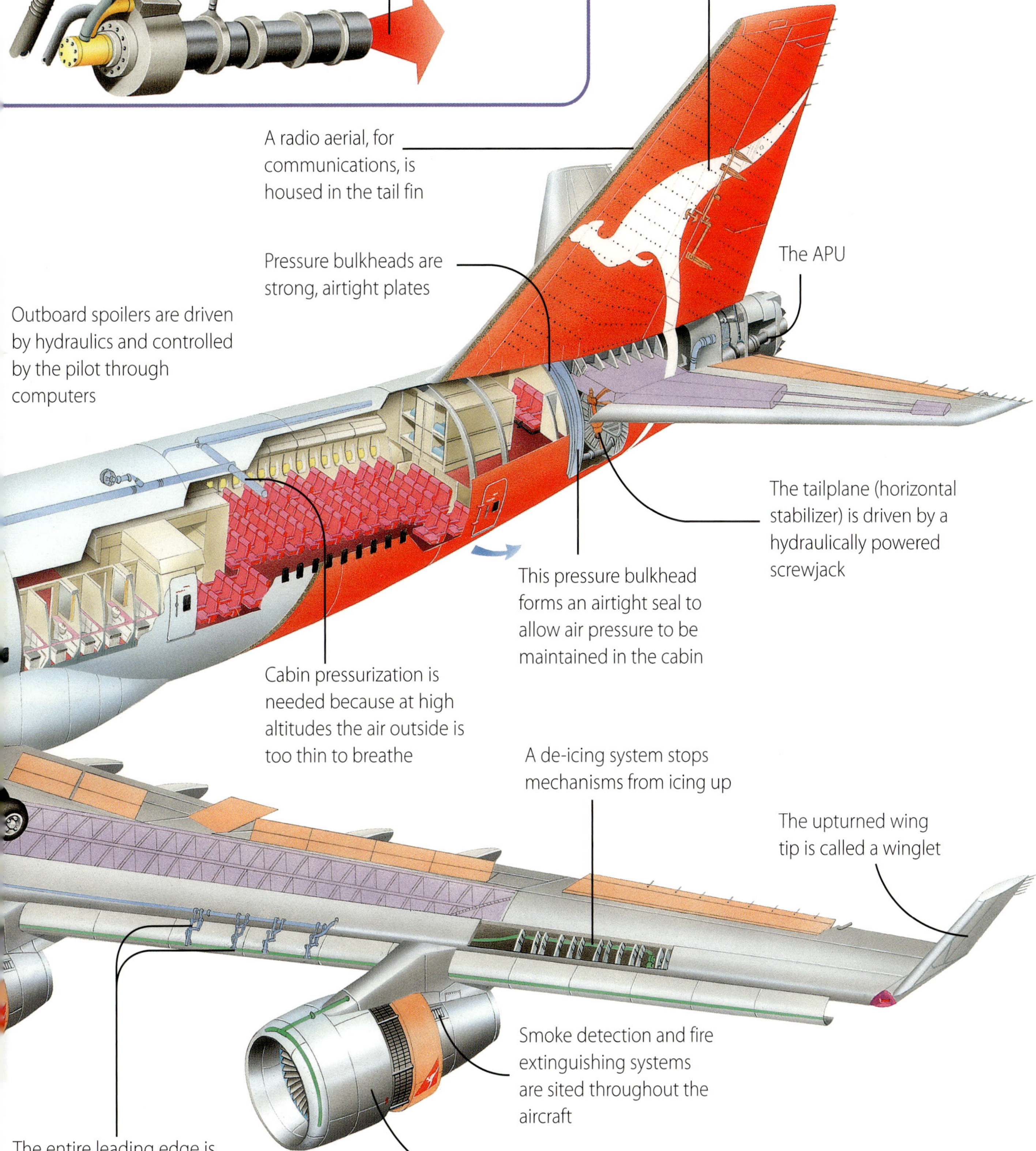
The logo of the airline is usually painted on the tail fin
A radio aerial, for communications, is housed in the tail fin
Pressure bulkheads are strong, airtight plates
The APU
Outboard spoilers are driven by hydraulics and controlled by the pilot through computers
The tailplane (horizontal stabilizer) is driven by a hydraulically powered screwjack
This pressure bulkhead forms an airtight seal to allow air pressure to be maintained in the cabin
Cabin pressurization is needed because at high altitudes the air outside is too thin to breathe
A de-icing system stops mechanisms from icing up
The upturned wing tip is called a winglet
Smoke detection and fire extinguishing systems are sited throughout the aircraft
The entire leading edge is movable – it is driven by powerful hydraulic rams
Each of the four engines weighs about 5.5 tons (5 mt)

Air Traffic Control

Like cars on a road, aircraft have to be controlled and obey rules in order to avoid midair collisions. Large and powerful aircraft keep to invisible "roads" called airways. Controllers work from a control tower (*right*) and can watch the progress of each aircraft on radar screens. They can tell which aircraft is which, at what altitude they are flying, and where they are heading. Each aircraft has its own navigation systems to guide it, and stations on the ground, called VORs, act like airway signposts. When an aircraft reaches its destination, it may have to join a stack (a queue) to await its turn to be guided down to the runway.

ILS

The ILS (instrument landing system) enables aircraft equipped with an ILS receiver to land safely, even in low cloud and fog. It consists of two radio beams, sent from near the runway towards approaching aircraft. One guides the aircraft's direction (left or right). The other guides it vertically (up or down) along the correct glide path.

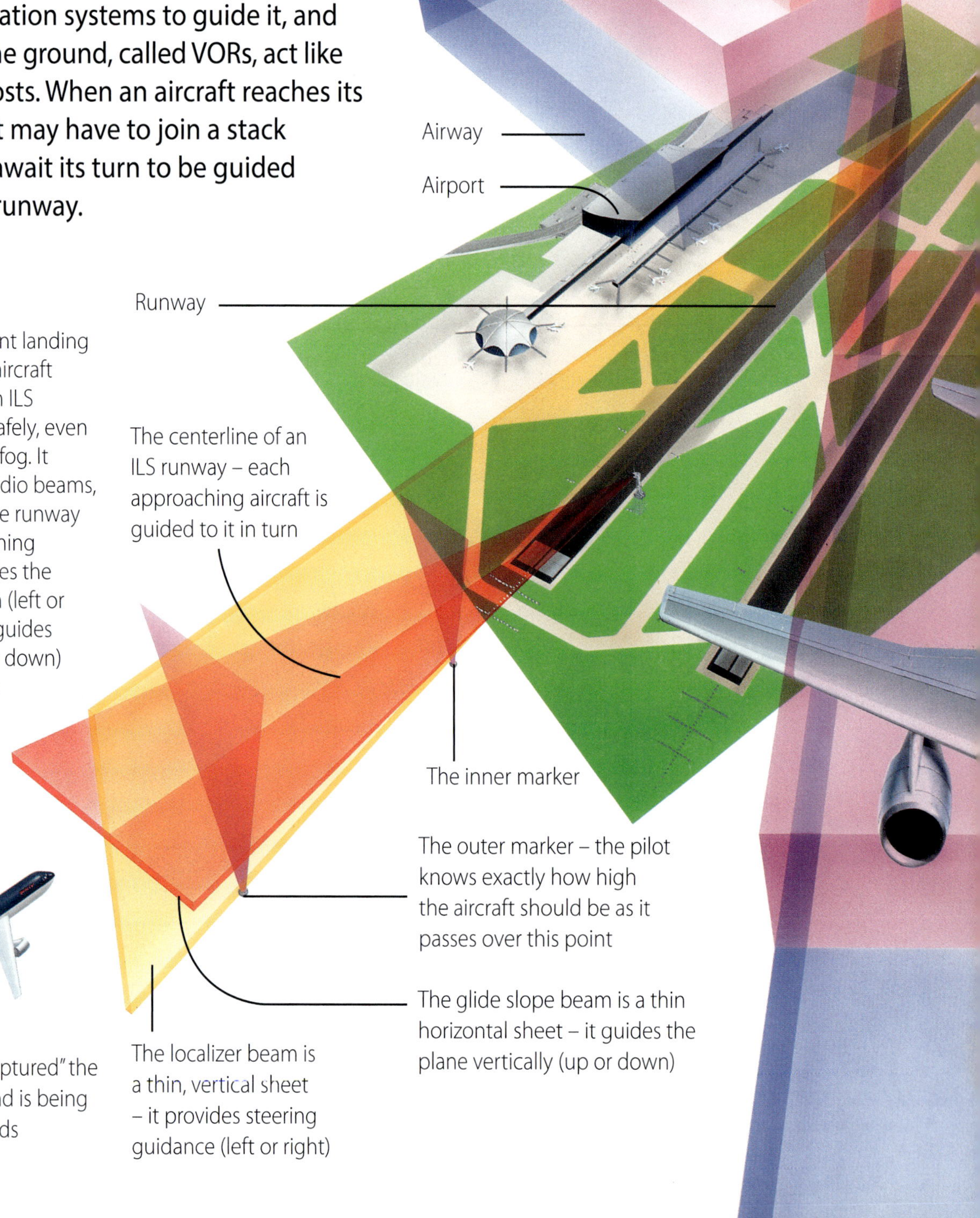

Stacking

When aircraft are queued, they join the stack at the top and fly around in circles, gradually losing height, until air traffic control allow them to make their landing approach.

GPS and satnav

Most modern aircraft are fitted with GPS receivers. These use the Global Positioning System of satellites that orbit Earth and send out coded radio signals. A GPS receiver uses the signals from three or more satellites to calculate its position with an accuracy of 50 feet (15 m) or less. GPS is sometimes called satnav (satellite navigation).

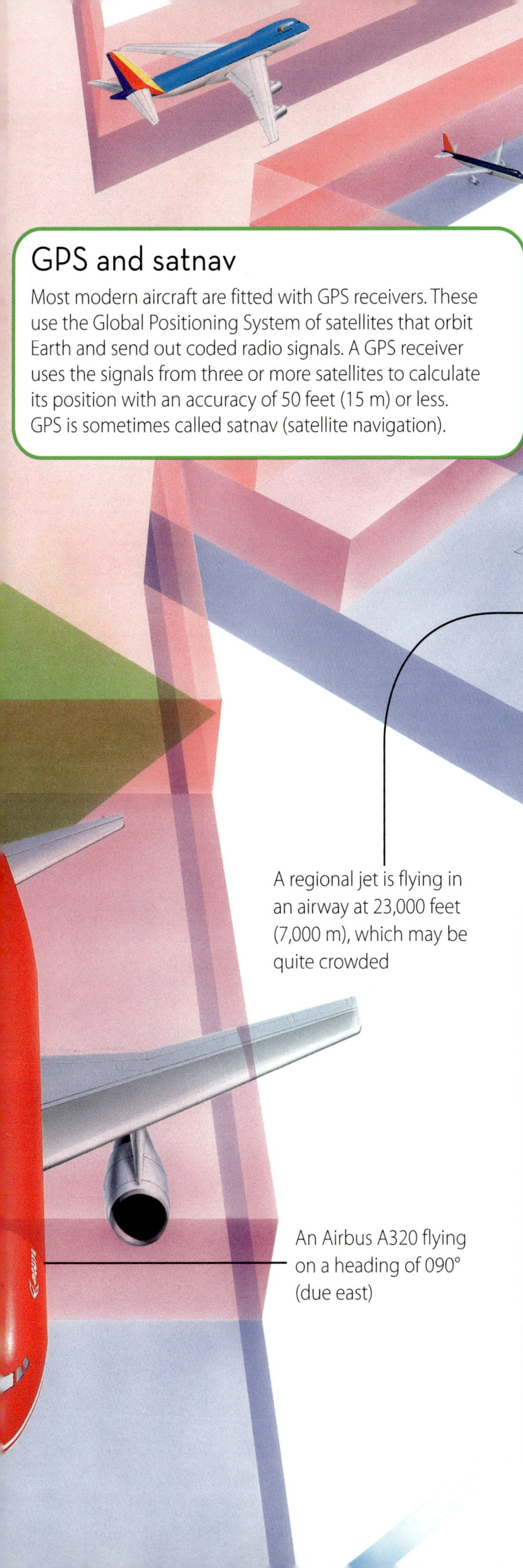

VOR

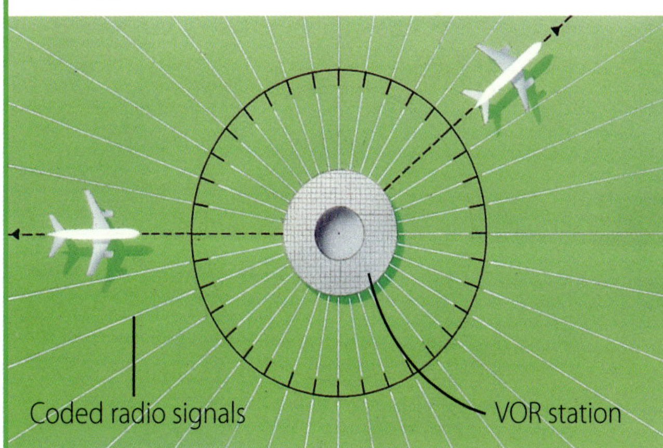

Thousands of radio stations called VORs (very high frequency omni-directional radio range) are in 24-hour use all over the world. Each one sends out coded radio signals in every direction, like the spokes of a wheel. They tell all aircraft the direction to each VOR, helping pilots to find their way (navigate). Modern airliners do not need to use VOR stations, as they have their own GPS-based navigation systems.

Radar

Radar uses special radio beams to detect objects at a great distance, even at night or through clouds. Huge radar stations on the ground monitor the progress of every aircraft in the sky for hundreds of miles (km) in all directions. Most big or powerful aircraft carry their own radar. The main radar will be in the nose, looking ahead like a car headlight. A passenger jet's radar scans the flight path for mountains, for other aircraft at the same height (to avoid them), and especially for thunderstorms and clouds, which could toss the aircraft around and make passengers feel airsick. By checking the radar screens, the pilot is able to "see" far ahead and steer around turbulence (stormy air), even at night.

Fighters and bombers often have a backward-facing radar as well, to warn if an enemy fighter is trying to approach them from behind. There are also special radars that can produce a detailed picture of the ground below the aircraft.

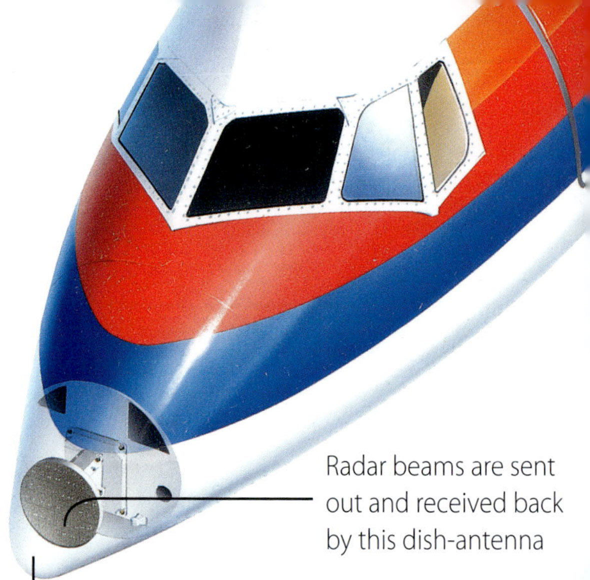

Radar location

The most common place for an aircraft's radar is in its nose. From here it is able to scan the horizon to detect obstacles or bad weather ahead of the aircraft.

Radar altimeter

Ordinary altimeters measure air density, which decreases with height. However, these cannot tell if an aircraft at an altitude of 1,000 feet (300 m) is heading towards a 2,000-foot (600 m) mountain. A radar altimeter measures the exact distance to the ground and would detect the rising land level of the mountain.

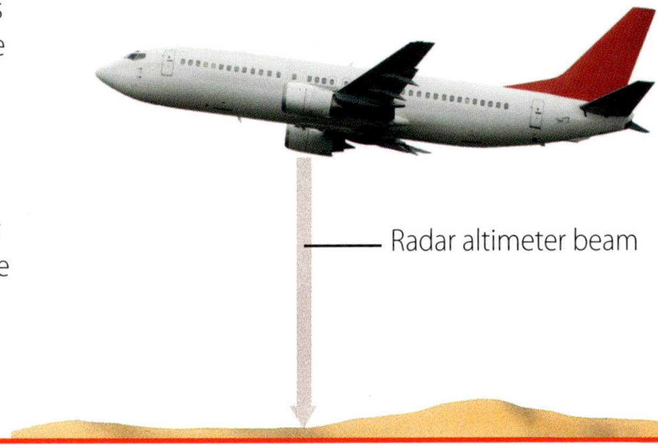

Analog radar altimeter display

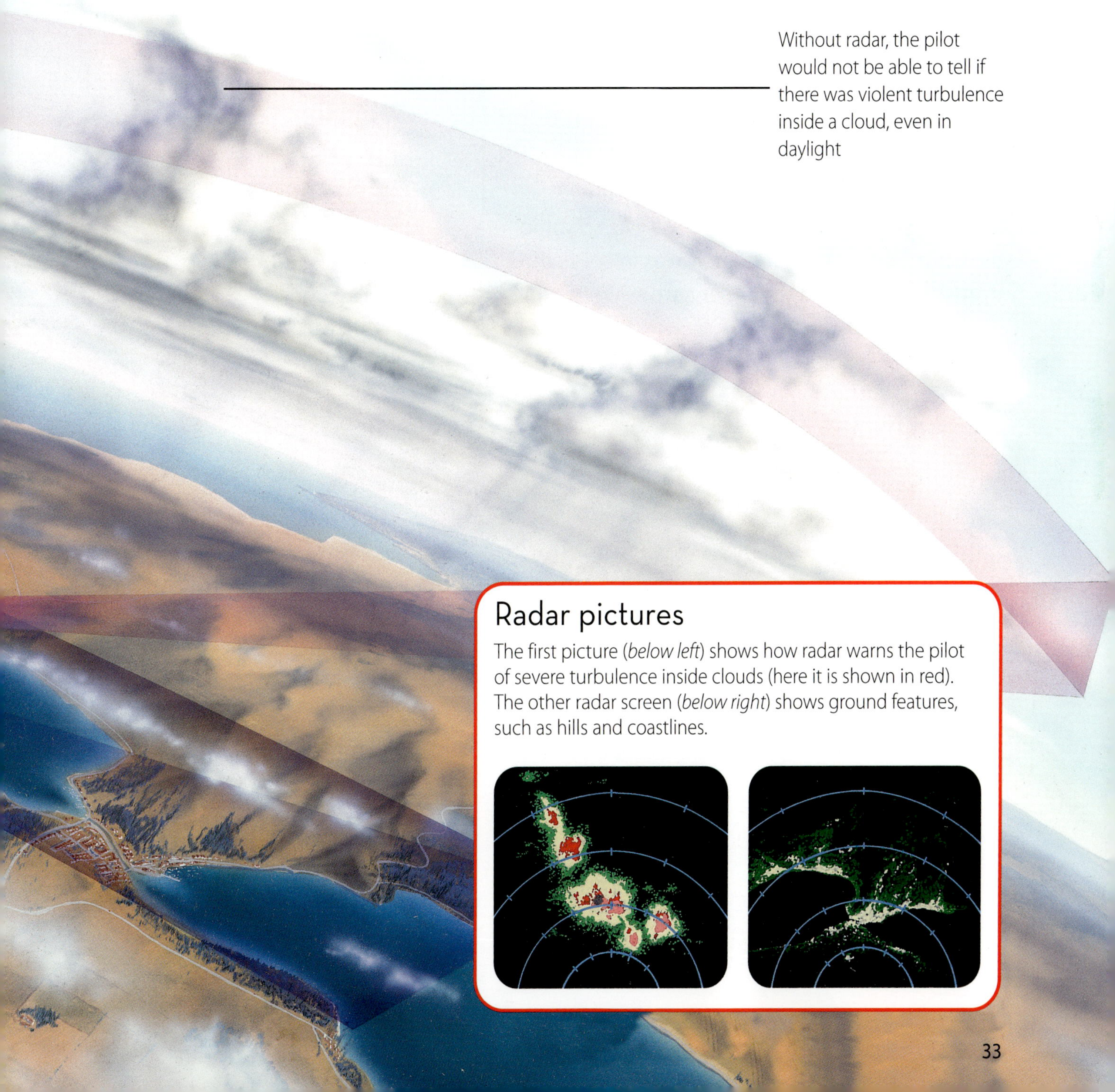

Radar pictures

The first picture (*below left*) shows how radar warns the pilot of severe turbulence inside clouds (here it is shown in red). The other radar screen (*below right*) shows ground features, such as hills and coastlines.

Supersonic Aircraft

Sound travels through the air at a speed of about 761.2 miles per hour (1,225 kph). In 1947, an American, Chuck Yeager, piloted the first airplane able to fly faster than sound. Aircraft able to do this are called supersonic. In 1959, an X-15 airplane (*below*) made its first flight. Powered by a rocket, and with only one man aboard, the X-15 was capable of reaching speeds of up to 4,520 mph (7,274 kph), or nearly seven times the speed of sound. This speed was achieved in October 1967 and is still the fastest recorded manned flight, although in 2004 an unmanned NASA X-43A scramjet reached a speed of 7,545.9 mph (12,144 kph). In 1969, the first Concorde was built – it was designed to be the world's first SST (supersonic transport) passenger aircraft. It was in service from 1976 to 2003 and 20 Concordes were built.

Subsonic flight

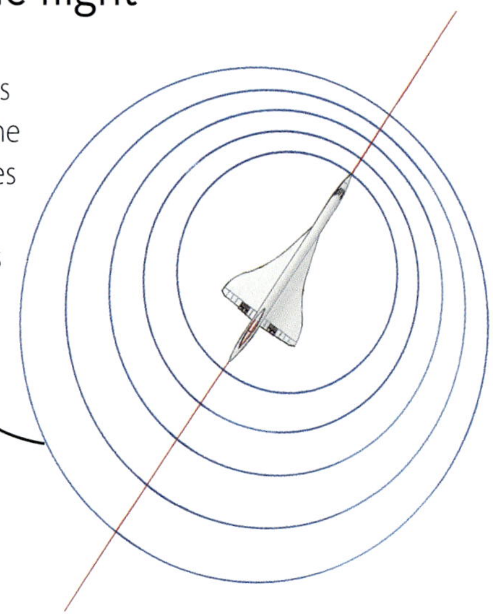

The diagram above shows how the Concorde supersonic airliner flew at subsonic speed (slower than sound). The sound waves spread away like ripples on a pond, those in front of the nose traveling away from it. This happens with all subsonic aircraft. The noise of their engines rushes away from them much faster than they can fly.

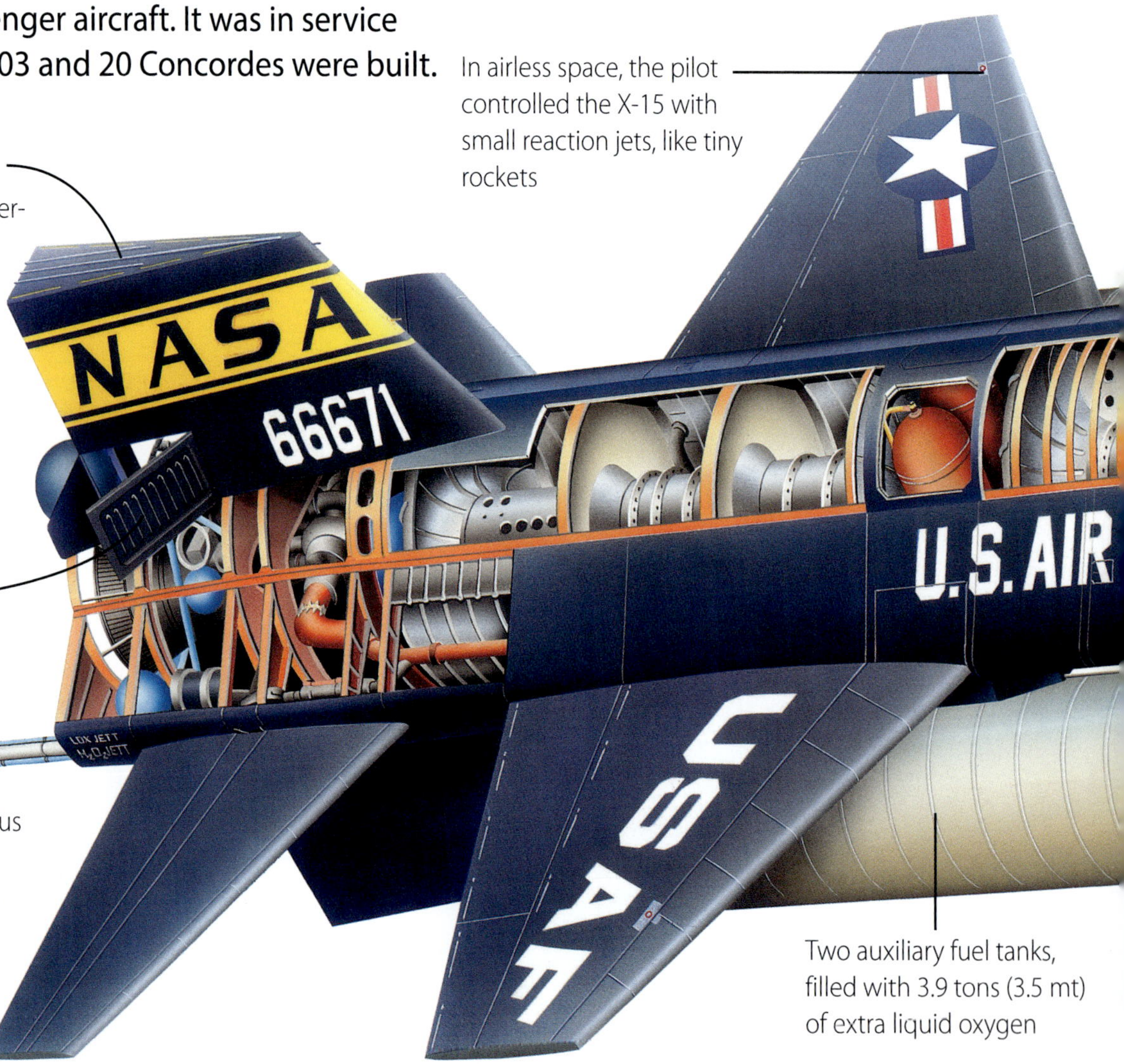

At the speed of sound

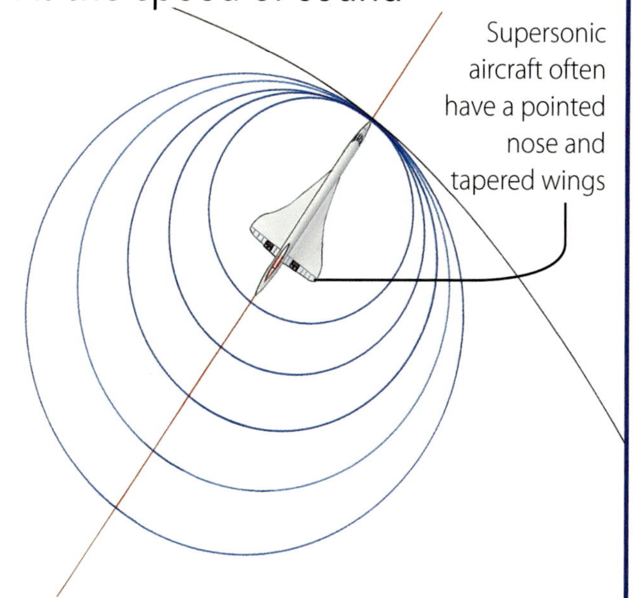

This diagram shows how Concorde flew at Mach 1, which is exactly the same speed as sound. All the aircraft's sound waves bunched together at the nose. The aircraft moved forward at the same speed as the waves themselves.

Mach 2

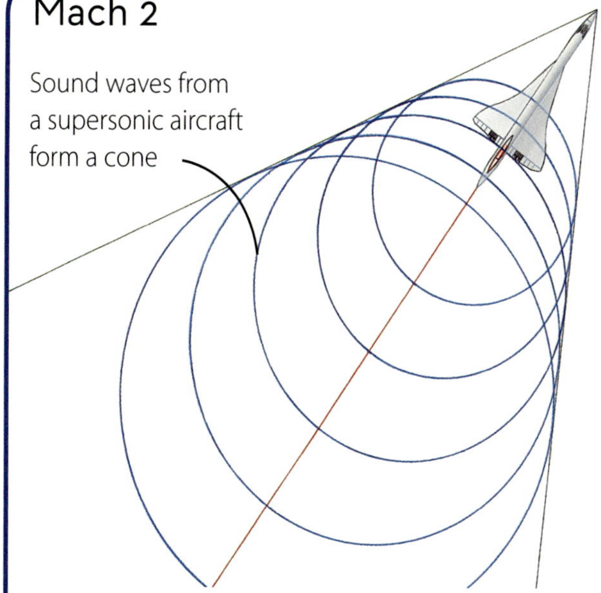

Concorde's cruising speed was usually Mach 2 (twice as fast as sound). The aircraft's sound waves traveled at the same speed as before, but Concorde flew ahead much faster. Concorde was specially shaped so that its wings stayed within the sound waves and the pilot could keep control of the aircraft.

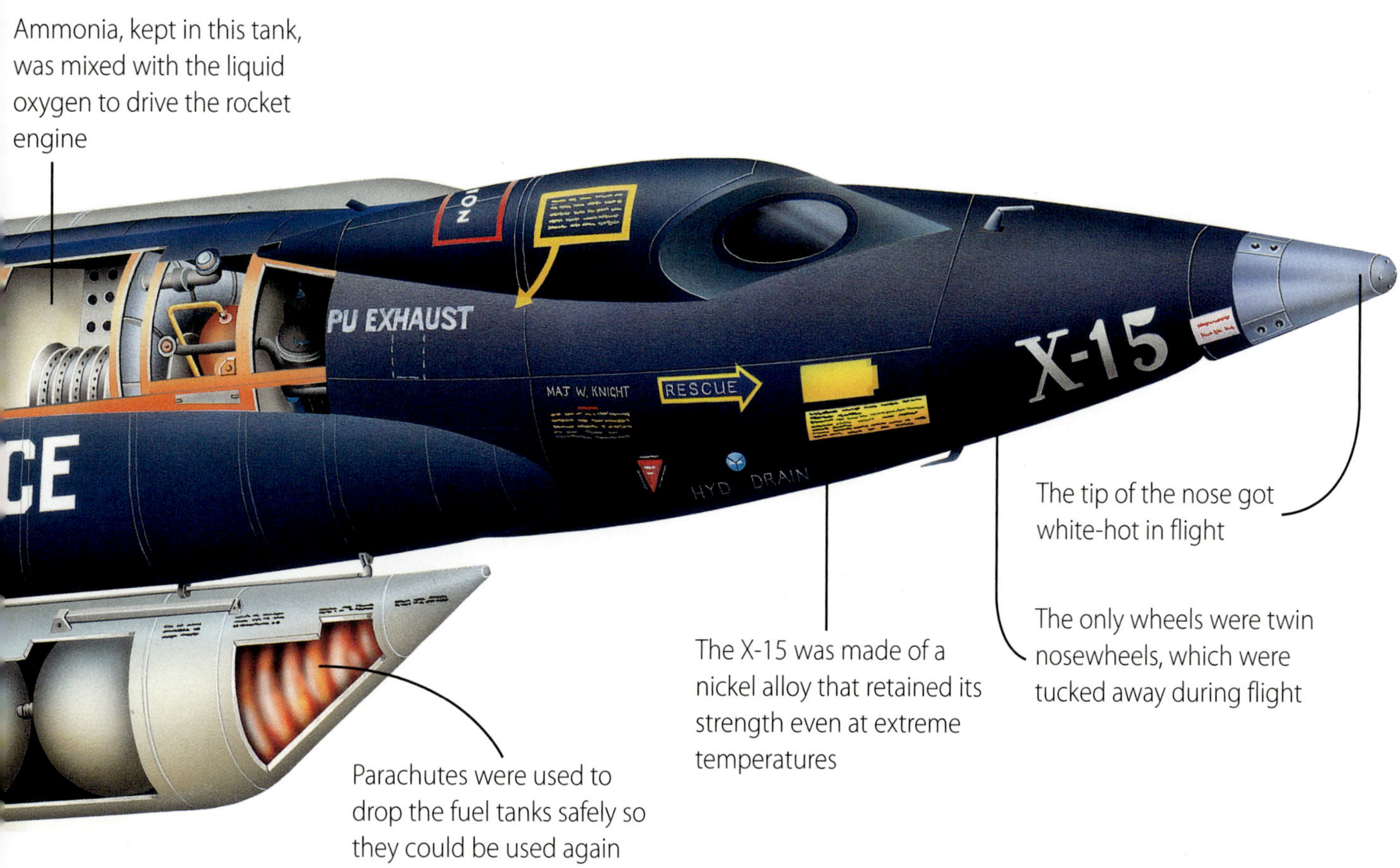

VTOL Aircraft

When taking off from the ground, ordinary airplanes have to travel down a long runway to build up enough speed for their wings to generate a lift greater than the aircraft's weight. Ordinary aircraft also need a runway in order to land safely.

Until 1960, only helicopters could perform vertical takeoff and landings in a small space without a runway. In 1960, a team of British engineers produced a prototype airplane with one jet engine with two nozzles on each side. The nozzles could be rotated to point downwards to give the aircraft lift, or backwards to power the aircraft forward in normal flight. This allowed it to perform vertical takeoff and landing, or VTOL. This led to the development of the unique Harrier (*right*), often called the "Jump Jet." It first flew in 1967 and remains the only true VTOL warplane. Some Harriers are used by Naval Air Forces and are based on aircraft carriers.

Harrier and V-22 Osprey

The Harrier (*right, top*) has a special turbofan engine with four nozzles, two on each side. These can swivel and point down to lift the Harrier. When they point backwards, they can drive it forward at almost the speed of sound. The V-22 Osprey (*bottom left and right, bottom*) can also land and take off vertically. It has two big prop rotors. When they are tilted up, they act like rotors and lift the Osprey. When tilted forwards, they act like propellers and pull it at 310 mph (500 kph). The Osprey can do everything a helicopter can do, but it can fly twice as fast and more than twice as far.

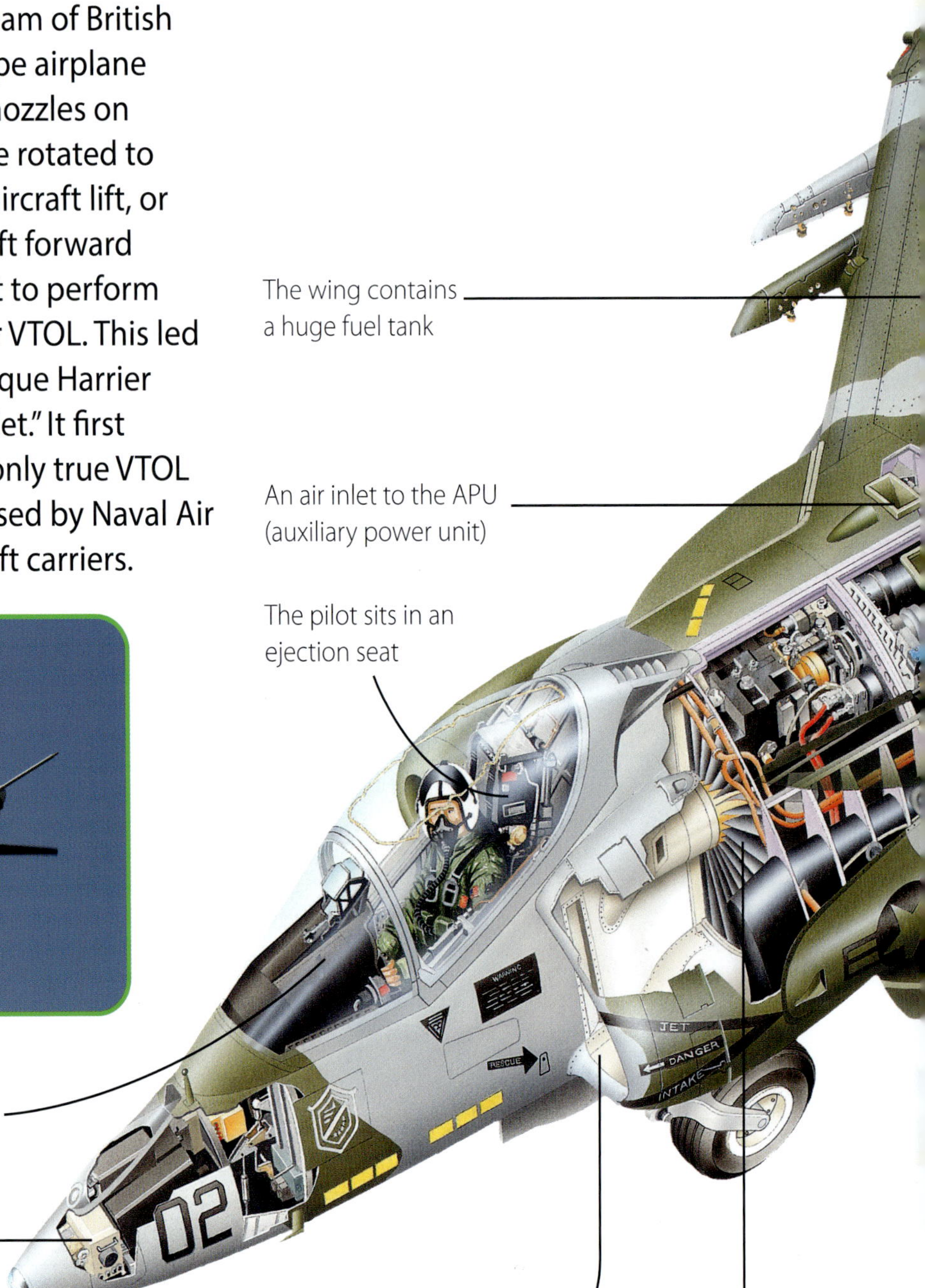

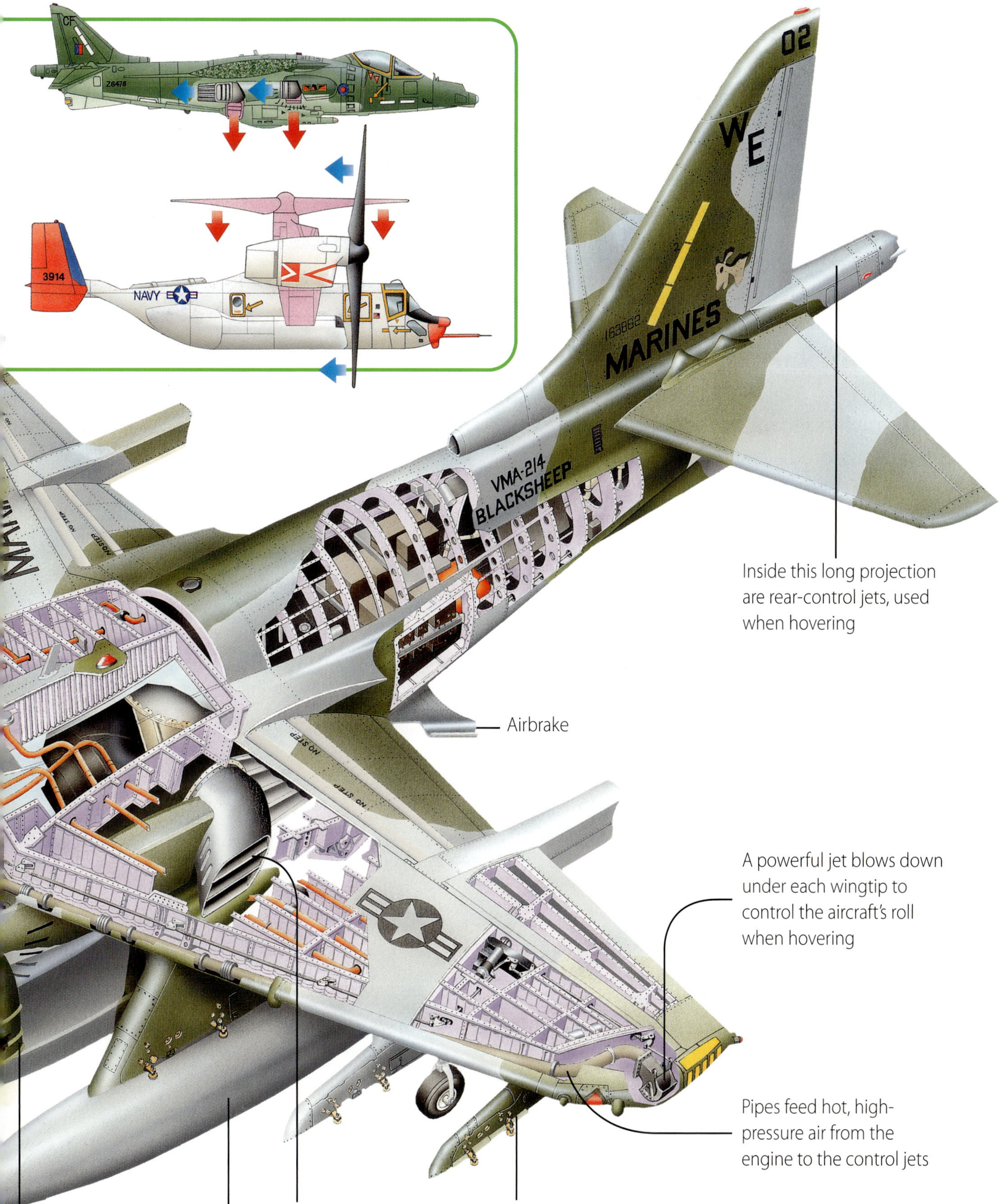
CF
NAVY
3914
02
WE
MARINES
VMA-214
BLACKSHEEP
NO STEP
Inside this long projection are rear-control jets, used when hovering
Airbrake
A powerful jet blows down under each wingtip to control the aircraft's roll when hovering
Pipes feed hot, high-pressure air from the engine to the control jets
One of the two rear nozzles which discharge the hot jet from the engine
Racks are used to carry fuel tanks or weapons
A front engine nozzle – shown here in the vertical-lift position
An auxiliary fuel tank, which holds more than 317 gallons (1,200 l)

Microlights

Since the early days of flight, many designers have tried to create small, affordable light aircraft. Around 1960, a new kind of wing, called the Rogallo, was introduced which made the now popular sport of hang gliding possible. It was shaped like a triangle, flying point-first. A light framework of metal tubing was added underneath to support a person's weight.

Such gliders led in turn to the development of small powered airplanes, or "microlights." The pilot sits on or inside a tiny craft with a pusher engine at the back. Some of these microlights still have Rogallo wings, but today most have simple rigid wings. The modern "micro" consists of a wing and a "trike unit" (named for its three wheels). Autogyros, which have a rotor instead of a wing, have also been developed. These are powered by a small engine which drives a propeller at the back of the autogyro. The aircraft's forward motion causes air to rush past the rotor blades, spinning them around and creating lift.

Autogyros

The autogyro was invented by Spanish engineer Juan de la Cierva in an attempt to create an aircraft that could fly safely at low speeds. He first flew one on January 9, 1923, at Cuatro Vientos Airfield in Madrid. The pilot sat in a streamlined pod with an open cockpit, like the one above, where a helmet and goggles were necessary. Pilots of other modern autogyros, where the cockpit is contained, still wear helmets for their safety.

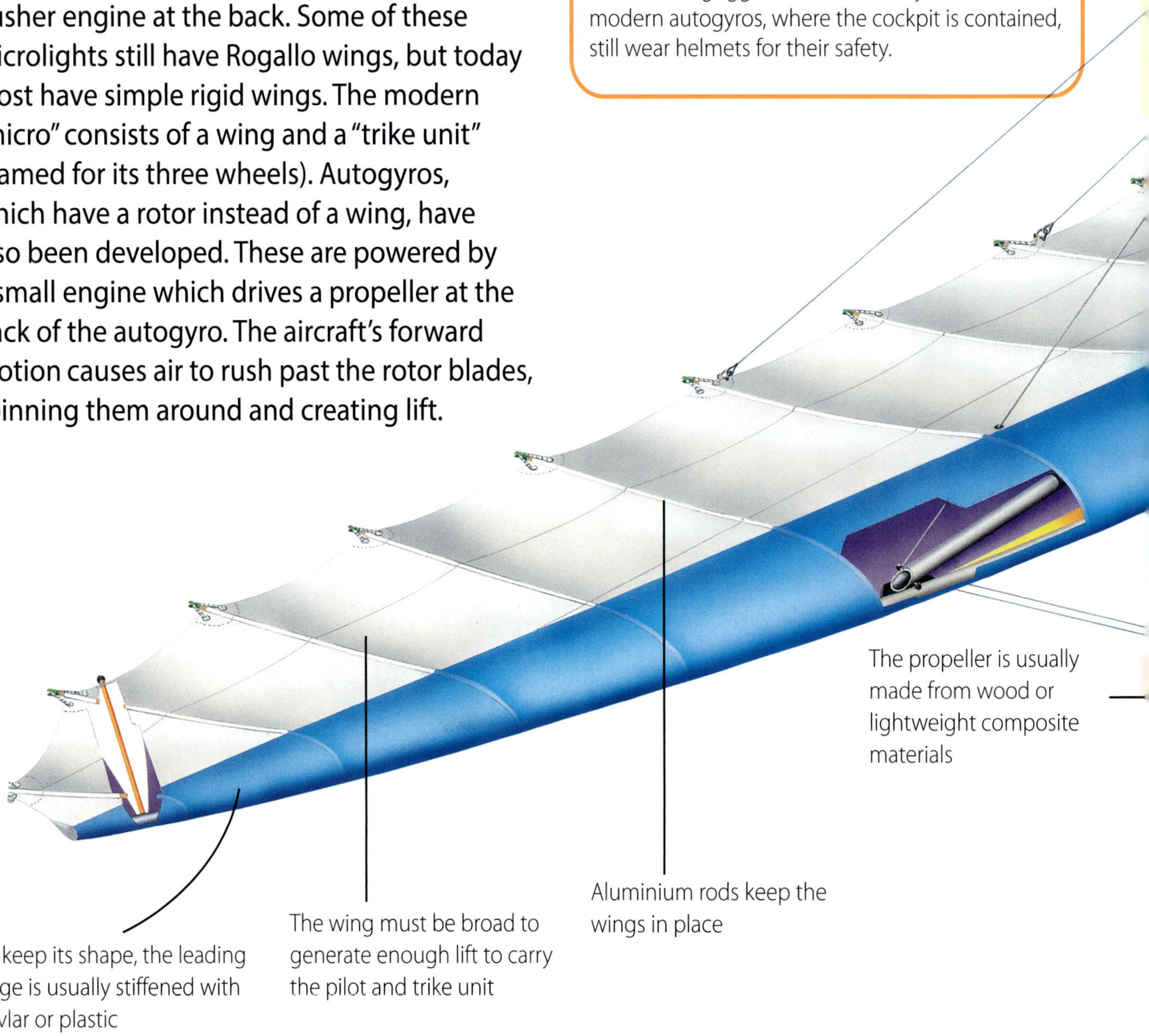

Cords attach each of the wing rods to the trailing edge
The rudder is used to steer the micro in the right direction
The wing and trike unit join at the A-frame
Strong wires or cables support the weight of the trike and pilot
The micro is controlled mainly by maneuvering the A-frame
Some micros can carry a passenger as well as the pilot
The small piston engine develops up to 100 horsepower
The wheels have brakes to stop the micro on the ground
PEGASUS
Sprung shock absorbers on the main wheels help to give a soft landing
The trike unit is usually made of fiberglass
This nose gear can be steered on the ground

Human-Powered Aircraft

The first human-powered aircraft was flown in 1961, for a distance of 2,132.5 feet (650 m). Designs and flight distances have since improved greatly, as lighter but stronger materials – such as titanium, carbon fiber, glass fiber, low-density plastic foam, and thin transparent film – have become available. The wing must have an enormous span, around 100 feet (30 m) from tip to tip, but be very light. The pilot must pedal to gain enough speed to take off, driving the large propeller through rotating shafts and gear wheels. A champion cyclist is needed if a human-powered aircraft is to be flown a long way. The *Daedalus*, shown here, holds the distance record for human-powered flight – 74 miles (119 km).

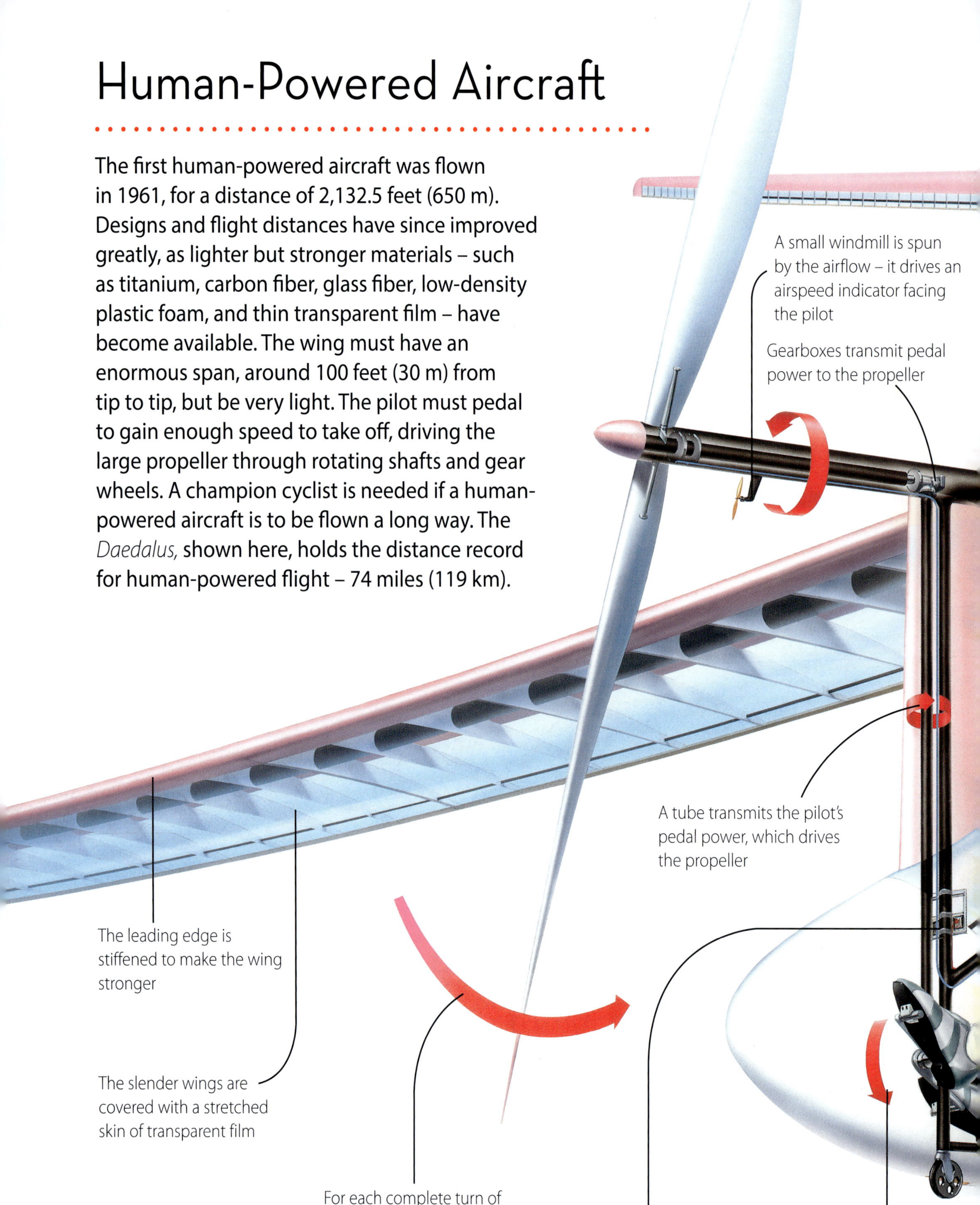

Daedalus

Every human-powered aircraft has a long wingspan and light weight. Together, this makes them flimsy and prone to damage. The wingspan of the *Daedalus* was 112 feet (34.1 m).

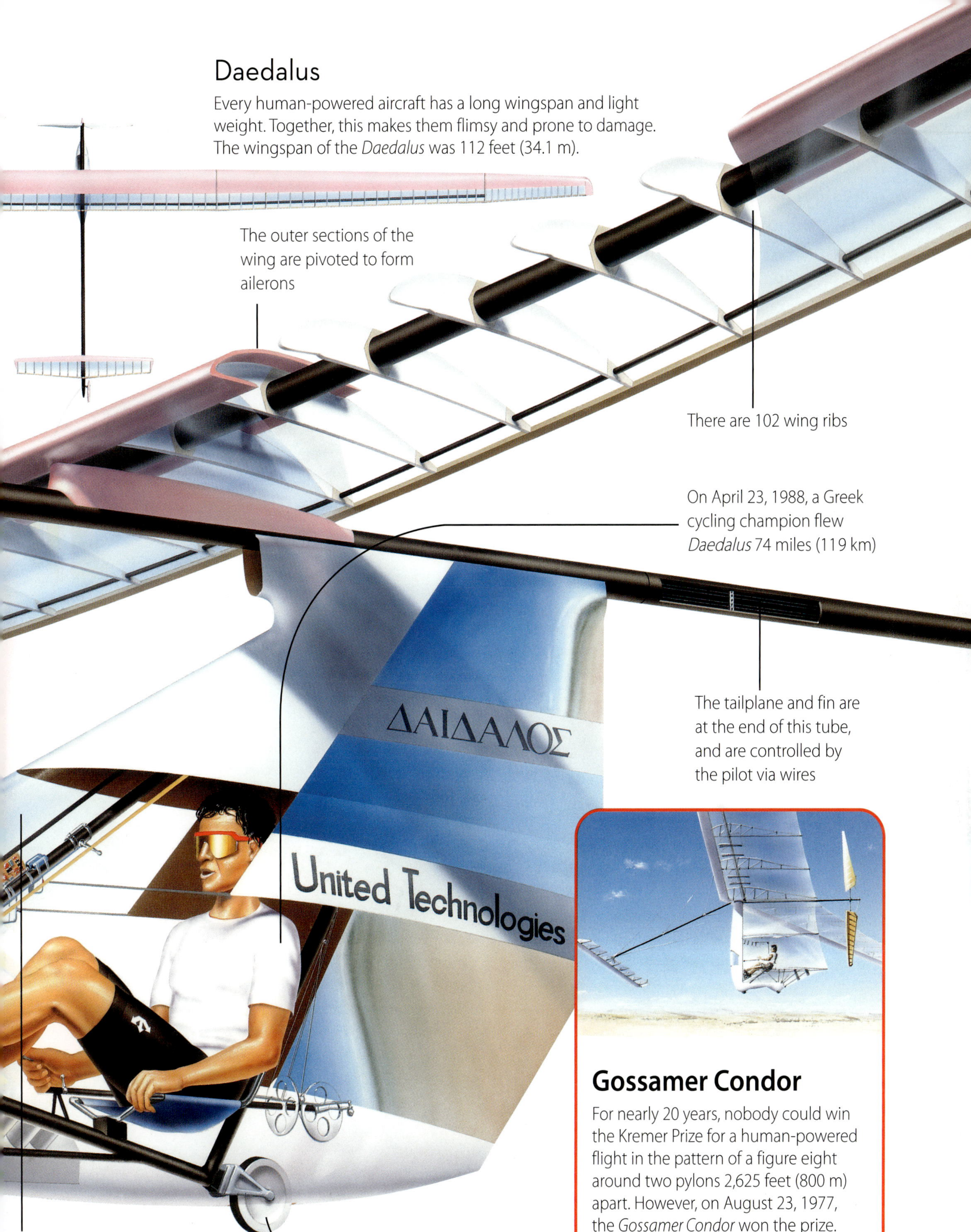

Gossamer Condor

For nearly 20 years, nobody could win the Kremer Prize for a human-powered flight in the pattern of a figure eight around two pylons 2,625 feet (800 m) apart. However, on August 23, 1977, the *Gossamer Condor* won the prize. One of its features was a foreplane instead of a rear tail.

Helicopter Flight

Helicopters do not appear to have wings. In fact, their wings are long and thin, and spin around and around, forming what is called a rotor. They are also called rotary-winged aircraft. This helicopter (*below*) is a Sikorsky Seahawk of the United States Navy, which first flew in 1974 and is still in active service. It has a four-blade main rotor: its four rotating wings lift it off the ground and propel it forwards or backwards. An upright rotor on the tail at the back pushes the tail sideways. This stops the main rotor from making the helicopter spin around and around. The rotors are driven by two powerful engines, one on each side of the helicopter's fuselage.

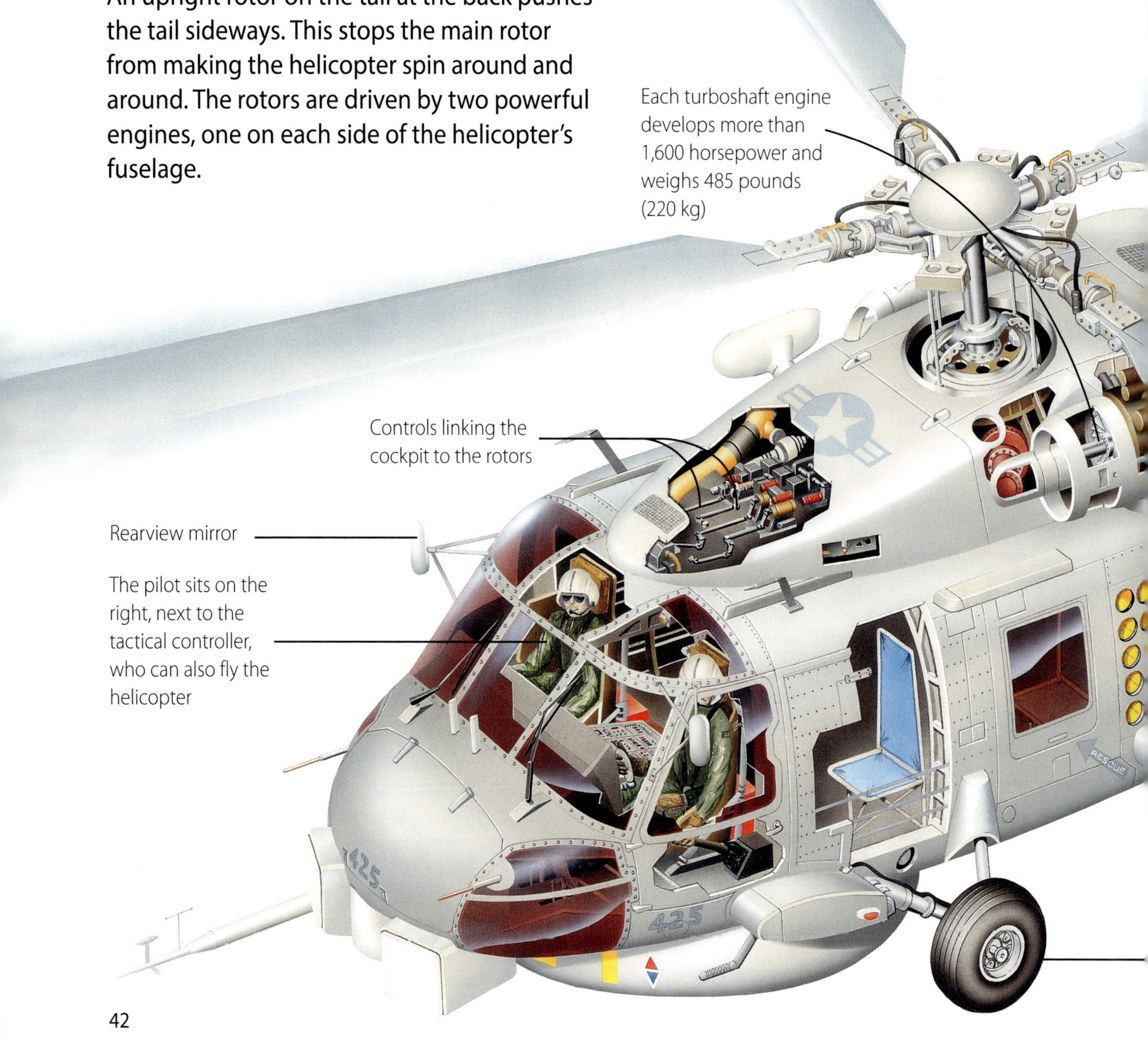